the reluctant traveler

the reluctant traveler

A Pilgrimage Through
Loss and Recovery

Diane Dempsey Marr, Ph.D.

NAVPRESS

Bringing Truth to Life
P.O. Box 35001, Colorado Springs, Colorado 80935

OUR GUARANTEE TO YOU

We believe so strongly in the message of our books that we are making this quality guarantee to you. If for any reason you are disappointed with the content of this book, return the title page to us with your name and address and we will refund to you the list price of the book. To help us serve you better, please briefly describe why you were disappointed. Mail your refund request to: NavPress, P.O. Box 35002, Colorado Springs, CO 80935.

The Navigators is an international Christian organization. Our mission is to reach, disciple, and equip people to know Christ and to make Him known through successive generations. We envision multitudes of diverse people in the United States and every other nation who have a passionate love for Christ, live a lifestyle of sharing Christ's love, and multiply spiritual laborers among those without Christ.

NavPress is the publishing ministry of The Navigators. NavPress publications help believers learn biblical truth and apply what they learn to their lives and ministries. Our mission is to stimulate spiritual formation among our readers.

ISBN 1-57683-271-6

Cover design by Kelly Noffsinger
Cover photography by Image Source/elektraVision/PictureQuest
Creative Team: Don Simpson, Greg Clouse, Nat Akin, Laura Spray, Pat Miller

Some of the anecdotal illustrations in this book are true to life and are included with the permission of the persons involved. All other illustrations are composites of real situations, and any resemblance to people living or dead is coincidental.

Unless otherwise identified, all Scripture quotations in this publication are taken from the *New American Standard Bible* (NASB), © The Lockman Foundation 1960, 1962, 1963, 1968, 1971, 1972, 1973, 1975, 1977, 1995.

Printed in the United States of America

1 2 3 4 5 6 7 8 9 10 / 06 05 04 03 02

FOR A FREE CATALOG OF
NAVPRESS BOOKS & BIBLE STUDIES,
CALL 1-800-366-7788 (USA)
OR 1-416-499-4615 (CANADA)

Dedication

In memory of my father, Robert Harold Dempsey, whose life-long portrayal of servanthood brought meaning and direction to my life. And to my mother, Emma Delia Dempsey, who continues to instruct me in the fine art of play.

Contents

Acknowledgments

I BELIEVE GOD made us to be relational beings, and as I review the names of people who have contributed in some way to this project, I am grateful for our inherent desire for connectedness. From the many people who shared their stories of loss and recovery with me, to those who energized the writing process with their enthusiasm or expertise, your gifts of love and support have been greatly appreciated. The encouragement received from the many wonderful people at NavPress transformed this project into a true blessing. In particular, I want to thank Don Simpson, whose willingness to consider the manuscript for publication allowed me to share my heart and vision for transforming life's challenges into tomorrow's wisdom. And to my editor, Greg Clouse, special thanks for the respect and honor he gave my personal story while providing valuable feedback that enriched the quality and depth of the workbook.

Dr. Dennis Sterner, Dean of the School of Education at Whitworth College, honored my desire to write by helping me clear a space in my academic schedule to make such work possible. Dr. Gordon Jackson assisted with the development of the proposal that was ultimately accepted by NavPress; and Dr. Linda Lawrence Hunt, Nancy Greinert, Dr. William Johnson, and Rachel Johnson critiqued the initial chapter accompanying that proposal.

And even though I had to swap him a batch of homemade chocolate chip cookies in exchange for critiquing the first three chapters of the manuscript, I still want to thank my stepson, Jason Marr, for his thoughtful remarks.

Psychologist Dr. Stephanie Tovey reviewed the therapeutic aspects of the workbook while Linda Anderson, my old college roommate and friend for almost thirty years, gave valuable feedback that helped me to put the final touches on the manuscript. Suzette McGonigal, Dr. Sharon Mowry, and Izzy RaLonde, having read the first draft of my manuscript from cover to cover, deserve special thanks for bringing encouragement, a sense of humor, and honest feedback to this project.

I also owe a debt of gratitude to my friends and Whitworth colleagues Drs. Barbara Sanders and Betty Williams, who shared their hearts, offered their prayers, celebrated my progress, and encouraged my desire to grow spiritually. It is a rare and wonderful gift to share my personal and professional life with these "Women of Purpose."

Finally, there are no words to express the affection and appreciation I have for the two special men with whom I share my life and home. My husband, Dargan, read each draft of the manuscript, provided love and encouragement when I felt stuck, and faithfully prepared wonderful meals to sustain me throughout the writing process. The biscotti weren't bad either! My dear son, Jacob, energized and enriched my life as only a teenager can, providing me with happy distractions after patiently waiting for Mom to take a break. Thank you, gentlemen!

Preface

THE SUMMER OF 1996 signaled the end to my family's sojourn in the Midwest. I had accepted a new professorship that would transport us back to the Pacific Northwest, and although jubilant about returning home, I had to contend with several difficult but typical loss issues that occur as a result of relocation. I said good-bye to my dream home, a lower cost of living, a wonderful church family, a daughter now grown, and friends whom I cherished. Waiting for me were the demands of reestablishment: finding a suitable home, creating a new support system, settling my son into a new school, and learning the duties of a new job. Although the upheaval was daunting, my husband and I felt certain that we had made the right decision. We were willing to wade through these losses and challenges, considering them well within the realm of normalcy.

We had barely unpacked the last box when a wave of catastrophic losses washed over my life and the lives of those I loved. As autumn colors signaled the fast-approaching snows, I bid farewell to a cousin and a friend, both claimed by the cruel realities of addiction. Only a few weeks later my brother, Michael, was diagnosed with an aggressive and rare form of cancer. The doctors offered little hope, predicting that within three months Michael would succumb to the disease. Despite our frantic efforts to uncover a viable treatment option, we played out the final scene as foretold by conventional medicine. Like a train without brakes, Michael headed for ultimate disaster. Early spring found us by his side as he labored to free himself of a physical body ravaged by cancer. And when it was over, all I had left were my memories—and a bittersweet pain that threatened to crush my soul.

To say that I struggled to go on living my life as normal would be an understatement. Time seemed to stand still as I fought to regain my balance. Words of comfort spoken by others seemed empty and meaningless. The only thing that was real to me was the pain that threatened to invade every aspect of my being. I prayed fervently to be spared from further challenges in a time when I felt so fragile, but even this was not to be.

Soon, in the midst of the summer's heat, I would fly to California to assist my parents and grandmother with medical and legal issues. I dreaded the reality of what waited for me. I had never been so clearly aware of my need for control until then, when my lack of it could no longer be denied. In my mind I have a vivid picture of that startling moment.

Only days after my brother had died it became clear that my father was gravely ill. I knew in my heart that time was short and soon I would be a fatherless daughter. The moment of truth came while on my knees, scrubbing my grandmother's kitchen floor. As tears streamed down my face I felt my lifelong foundation slip away. There was nothing I could do to prevent the erosive power of death from claiming yet another loved one. My only sibling was gone, my grandmother no longer knew who I was, and in the house next door my father, in a morphine haze, struggled as cancer's pain urged him to pace the floor. Even the family's nineteen-year-old cat looked as though he was ready to leave me an orphan. Less than four months after cancer had claimed my brother's life I stood at yet another bedside, this time holding the hand of my father as he drew his last breath.

In the midst of these sad events, colleagues recommended several books on grief recovery. Over the years, in my role as a psychotherapist, I had read my share of books on the subject and always welcomed new resources for my clients. This time, however, I would be reading to facilitate my own recovery. As I walked across campus to the college bookstore to purchase a copy of one of the books, I silently recalled the story I was told about that author's personal experience with grief. Having lost three family members in one horrific and senseless car accident, surely he possessed intimate knowledge of the pain and anguish I was experiencing.

I was not disappointed. Over the next several months I voraciously consumed a number of books dealing with personal stories of loss and academic discussions of grief recovery. Doing so helped me to gain fresh insight into the depths of my grief and a new sense of wonder for everyday life.

The creation of this workbook was inspired by my own personal journey through loss and the ongoing process of recovery, and my appreciation for the therapeutic benefits I reaped from various books on the subject. I also had another source of inspiration. In the summer of 1998 I had the privilege of facilitating a therapy group for seven courageous and amazing women who had suffered various forms of abuse and neglect as children. The depth of loss and the years of darkness experienced by these survivors highlighted for me the resiliency of the human spirit. Although they struggled with unfathomable pain, they also celebrated each step toward wholeness, however small it was. I gave each woman a copy of one of my favorite grief recovery books and suggested several more; in turn, they enthusiastically encouraged me to develop a companion workbook.

Although it can stand alone, I suggest that this workbook be used in conjunction with the recommended reading to facilitate a greater understanding of the recovery experience and to better promote personal healing. Because each person will travel his or her unique path to healing, I encourage readers to be sensitive to their individual needs.

Several factors should govern the use of the workbook and its exercises. For example, the amount of emotional energy available for working through issues of loss or the degree of readiness to explore them will impact the pace at which chapters are completed. Also, the reader may desire to use this as an individual journaling process or choose to utilize the workbook while receiving therapeutic support from a licensed professional counselor or licensed psychologist. A final consideration is the order in which chapters are read. Readers interested in developing a self-care plan or locating helpful grief recovery resources will find an array of suggestions in chapter 8 and appendix C. Regardless of the path chosen, it is important to remember that there is no right or wrong way to use this workbook.

Dealing with catastrophic loss is no easy matter. But even in the tangle of emotions, the difficult changes, and the darkness that pervades the moment, there remains the possibility of a richer and more meaningful existence. I believe this is made possible through divine grace. God continues to unfold before me the magnificence of His love and the depth of His commitment to humankind. In this time of my life, more than any other, I have come to a deeper understanding of how precious we are to Him. May the challenges and celebrations of future days bless each of you with such knowledge.

Difficult Farewells

Identifying and Naming Our Loss

The LORD is near to the brokenhearted
And saves those who are crushed in spirit.
(PSALM 34:18)

The Road Ahead

With the exception of overt tragedies such as death or natural disaster, today's fast-paced world allows little time for reflection, actual grieving, or integration of loss. Encouraged to get on with the business of life, many of us rush ahead of the natural grieving process in hopes of avoiding inevitable pain and the inconvenience it is likely to bring. Taking time to grieve would, at best, risk our being viewed as weak or melodramatic; or at worst, jeopardize our reputation should we be judged as irresponsible in the execution of daily responsibilities. As a result, isolation, depression, and loneliness become constant traveling companions for many of us.

Others of us allow loss and its subsequent pain to ravenously eat away at daily life, robbing us of any lasting pleasure and requiring constant attention to wounds that never quite heal. We often feel fragile, damaged, and cheated, which show up in behaviors of anger, resentment, bitterness, and self-pity. We wonder why God has abandoned us in our hour of greatest need. Loss becomes the proverbial "ball and chain," not only for us but also for those who care about us.

Learning to cope effectively with catastrophic loss is central to enjoying a robust and meaningful life. Unresolved grief is thought to be a contributing factor to numerous human challenges, including poor physical health, low self-esteem, depression, anxiety, unsatisfactory relationships, and poor work performance. Rather than act as an inescapable deterrent to healthy functioning, loss can instead be used to enrich and deepen our appreciation for life and living. To accomplish this transformation we must equip ourselves with knowledge, insight, and practical tools to travel the long road ahead. We need to find peace in the midst of difficult spiritual questions that seem to have no easy answers. In addition, we need a means by which we can identify our loss, understand and experience the grieving process, and redefine our personhood as we integrate loss into daily life. That is what this workbook is about. Completing the recommended readings and engaging in the workbook's exercises will help open the door to healing, integration, and restoration.

Definitions

It might be helpful to first clarify the meaning of terms we will be using throughout this workbook. According to the *American Heritage Dictionary, catastrophe* can be defined as:

> a great, often sudden calamity;
> a complete failure.

The term *loss* is defined as:

> the condition of being deprived or bereaved of something or someone;
> the harm or suffering caused by losing or being lost;
> destruction.[1]

Personalizing these terms allows us to bring a deeper meaning to our unique experience of loss. In his book *A Grace Disguised,* Dr. Gerald Sittser defined his perspective on *catastrophic loss* in the following manner:

> Catastrophic loss wreaks destruction like a massive flood. It is unrelenting, unforgiving, and uncontrollable, brutally erosive to body, mind, and spirit.[2]

Create a definition for *catastrophic loss* based on your life experience.

Describe the feelings that surfaced as you personalized the definition.

Purchase a large spiral-bound sketchbook that can serve as your creative journal. In your sketchbook draw a picture or create a collage that represents the feelings you just described.

How Loss Manifests Itself

Catastrophic loss transcends socioeconomic and cultural boundaries. It shows no respect for gender, age, or temperament and rarely consults us with regard to timing or our ability to cope. This monster shows no preference for fresh adventure, consistency, or logic. It has been known to stalk some of us frequently while barely noticing others. On occasion, sneaking up without warning, it can catch us unprepared for the chaos it leaves in its wake. At other times we may feel as though we are being held tightly in the monster's grip, made to watch the devastation unfold in slow motion as we remain immobile and powerless to effect change. Catastrophic loss is like the chameleon that can change its colors or the amoeba able to alter its shape. It is predictably unpredictable, possessing the ability to mold itself around any number of unfortunate circumstances.

Here are some examples of how *catastrophic loss* can manifest itself:

- ► Accident
- ► Adoption
- ► Birth of a disabled child
- ► Death
- ► Disability
- ► Divorce
- ► Illness
- ► Loss of a dream
- ► Loss of home
- ► Loss of a job
- ► Loss of lifestyle
- ► Loss of a significant relationship
- ► Loss of status
- ► Loss or death of a pet
- ► Mental illness
- ► Natural disaster
- ► Neglect
- ► Physical abuse
- ► Rape
- ► Severe emotional trauma
- ► Sexual abuse
- ► Underemployment

Review your own personal experience and perhaps interview a few friends or family members. Record below other examples of catastrophic loss of which you have become aware.

List the loss, or losses, you wish to work through as you complete this workbook.

It is not unusual for a primary loss to trigger additional losses in other areas of a person's life. You may have noticed this when you were recording your list. One loss seems to open many doors to others. Consider the example below.

Cascade of Loss

Primary Loss: CHRONIC UNDEREMPLOYMENT

- Secondary Losses: Loss of a lifestyle (no more eating out or nice vacations)
  - Loss of a home (you are unable to make mortgage payments, so you move into an apartment)
    - Loss of a pet (the apartment manager does not allow dogs in your building)
      - Loss of a dream (you had hoped that you would not have any money worries by age fifty)
        - Loss of status (working for an hourly wage does not carry the same prestige as the professional position you wanted)

It is difficult, if not impossible, to view loss as an isolated occurrence unrelated to other aspects of our life. In the preceding example, the primary loss (underemployment) created a cascade of loss across various aspects of existence. These losses not only impact the way we view ourselves and our circumstances, but also how we feel. For example, while underemployment and loss of status can have a negative impact on self-esteem (the evaluation we have of ourselves), loss of a pet can engender feelings of loneliness and depression.

Identify your primary loss, and then record the secondary losses that followed.

Your Cascade of Loss

Primary Loss:

Secondary Losses:

In light of these losses, describe what you believe to be true about yourself and your circumstances.

Describe the feelings you experience at seeing your own cascade of loss recorded on paper.

The common thread woven throughout the experience we define as *grieving* has the potential to link us with a caring community of others who bring empathic under-standing and compassion to our loss, warding off isolation and loneliness. Yet no two losses are alike. Although each incident of human loss may share with others a com-mon core of tasks in the grieving process, each loss requires us to navigate uncharted territory as well. For example, successfully coping with a death in your family does not necessarily mean that you can follow the same course in grieving the subsequent pass-ing of a loved one. Given that each loss is unique, there can be no magic formula. This also holds true when comparing individuals. Even though the outward appearance of loss may look similar—for example, both people have lost their spouses as a result of a car accident—the cascade of loss that follows will be unique to that surviving spouse's circumstances at the time of loss. In turn, personal attributes and resources will color the individual's ability to grieve and integrate loss. The moral of the story is to resist the temptation to base your expectations on your past experiences of loss or on the experiences of others, whether it involves:

- ► how you should grieve,
- ► what the grieving process itself should look like, or
- ► how long the grieving process should take.

Each loss will require you to embark on a distinct journey of healing.

Have there been times when you have been tempted to compare your loss to the loss of others?

In retrospect, what consequences did your comparisons have?

Embracing Our Loss

> I realized that I would have to suffer and adjust; I could not avoid it or escape it. There was no way out but ahead, into the abyss.[3] GERALD SITTSER

The initial step in any healing process is to recognize the need for healing. Regardless of the type or magnitude of our loss, we must first be willing and able to identify our loss as *loss*. This may seem ridiculously obvious, but let's pause for a moment to consider some examples of ways people may negate loss.

A newly divorced person throws a party and fails to grieve the loss of a significant relationship.

A rape victim believes it is her fault and allows silence to fuel her guilt and keep her walled off from help.

New parents tell themselves they should feel lucky that their disabled infant survived, but they fail to grieve the loss of their dreams for a "normal" child.

A widower believes that a "stiff upper lip" is the way to survive, keeping himself busier than usual to ward off a deep sense of grief.

A worker ignores the impact of being laid off because his situation is not as bad as someone else's.

Likely we know people who have somehow negated their losses; perhaps, without realizing it, we have done so ourselves. Ignoring, denying, or devaluing our loss prevents us from taking that first step in the healing process. Why then do people avoid naming their losses? Consider these primary reasons:

▶ We may be afraid that we will be overwhelmed by our pain.
▶ Guilt, shame, or remorse may be blocking our ability to view the experience as a loss.
▶ We may be afraid that we will lose our ability to function.
▶ We may feel humiliated and choose to deny that any loss has occurred.
▶ We may be afraid life will never be the same.

Write about the fears you may have in facing your loss.

In your sketchbook, draw a picture or create a collage that represents the feelings you had while exploring your fears.

To learn courage is to experiment with being courageous.[4] JUDY TATELBAUM

The desire to avoid pain is human nature. Reflex would have us search diligently for an alternative route leading us away from the experience of anguish. Yet avoidance prolongs the inevitable; it creates a tension between the desire to grow and move beyond the past and the need to resolve the past. Essentially we find ourselves stuck between what was and what we think should have been. This results in our past infecting, rather than enriching, our present and our future. It takes tremendous courage to face so daunting a task as coming to grips with the pain of loss. Fortunately, each of us possesses unique assets that not only support us throughout the grieving process, but also ensure that our life will ultimately be enhanced.

In your sketchbook, draw a picture or create a collage that represents the ambivalence you feel in attempting to avoid the pain of loss and your desire to continue to experience positive growth in your life.

About Resiliency

> Grace happens to me when I feel a surge of honest joy that makes me glad to be alive in spite of valid reasons for feeling terrible.[5] LEWIS SMEDES

More often than not, catastrophic loss pushes us to the brink of our coping abilities. The pilgrimage we are forced to embark on requires us to both accept and struggle with the inevitable pain while charting a course for a new and unknown land. How can we begin to prepare ourselves for what lies ahead when we feel so low? Discovering our resiliency traits may be one way to ready ourselves to contend with the challenges that await us.

Have you ever noticed how some people manage to bloom regardless of where they are planted? Psychologists who have studied this phenomenon of human nature have identified a number of characteristics that reflect this resiliency. According to the *American Heritage Dictionary, resiliency* can be defined as:

> the ability to recover quickly from illness, change, or misfortune.[6]

Resilient people tend to be optimists who, even in the midst of grief, look at life's challenges as opportunities to grow. They spend little time unearthing "whys" or extracting pity from others. They recognize resentment, bitterness, and unforgiveness as formidable barriers to experiencing life to its fullest. They are problem solvers who search for lessons in their experiences and apply what they have learned to future challenges. Resilient people view life as a dynamic process and thus strive to be flexible and willing to grow. They are open about their feelings and accept themselves and their experiences in the moment. These tenacious individuals embrace their own spirituality, gaining strength and meaning for their lives.

These traits help us weather the difficult and sometimes painful challenges of life. They do not alter the reality of our struggles, but they do shore us up in the midst of the storm. Seeds of resiliency are inside each of us, waiting to be nurtured so that we may glean the abundance of joy available even in the darkest of nights.

Below, in list form, are traits that reflect resiliency.

Able to identify feelings
Applies what is learned from experience in a positive way
Believes life is dynamic rather than static
Can vent painful feelings
Embraces spirituality
Flexible
Hopeful
Is a problem solver
Optimistic
Refuses to give up
Searches for meaning in experiences
Takes things in stride
Views change as a positive thing
Willing to work through even the most difficult of events

Make a list of the resiliency traits that have blossomed in your life. Feel free to add traits that do not appear on this list.

Describe an incident that reflects the presence of these traits in your life.

Make another list of the resiliency traits you wish to cultivate.

Choose one trait from your "wish" list and develop a plan that will help you cultivate it.

How and when will you get started?

Spiritual Reflection

> I know how to get along with humble means, and I also know how to live in
> prosperity; in any and every circumstance I have learned the secret of being
> filled and going hungry, both of having abundance and suffering need. I can
> do all things through Him who strengthens me. (PHILIPPIANS 4:12-13)

Gulping in the cool air of an early spring night, I stood outside the hospital where my
brother lay close to death. As I walked across the parking lot, scenes of the last twenty
hours flashed before me: the fear on Michael's face when he realized the end was near;
the urgency with which he shared final words with those he loved; his sweet spirit of
concern for those he would leave behind.

Michael clung tenaciously to life, fighting courageously for five months to gain vic-
tory over the cancer. He was not ready to die—he told me as much the day before he
passed away. I believe that we are made to hang onto life with every ounce of energy
we can muster. To do otherwise, to loosen our grip, seems unnatural. Yet this is what

God would have us do—let go of the trappings of this world.

In the months that followed the deaths of my brother and father, I often experienced an eerie sense of incompleteness. A piece of me was now gone and left a dark, empty void begging to somehow be filled. It became apparent that life, as I once knew it, had been fragile and temporary at best. What once was my foundation proved only to be dust, blown away by the hot, unrelenting winds of loss. Caught up were any illusions I once held about life's meaning. The pain and anguish that followed in the wake of my loss threatened to overwhelm me. It was at these times that I would hear the still, small voice of God speaking to my heart—*Diane, I am enough*—reassuring me that all was not lost.

Over many months, realization dawned slowly but surely as healing occurred. The teachable moments I experienced in my process of recovery continued to highlight one simple truth: God *is* enough. As I pondered the future without Michael in my life, God reminded me that, rather than depending on my brother, He would be the One by my side as I grew old. When I fretted over decisions where my father would have helped, God gently chided me to put them in His competent hands. Against the stark backdrop of unwanted change, I learned that God could meet my every need if only I would let Him. Until the moment I suffered great loss, I knew this truth only on an intellectual level. As my anguish subsided I began to understand with my heart. *He is enough!*

With each passing day I pray that this truth will sink deeper into my spirit. God is my brother, my Father, my family. He is our security, our Rock, our Comforter. He is all we need!

Describe your relationship with God.

What strength do you receive from your spiritual life?

What challenges are you facing spiritually as you begin to deal with your loss?

List three people you can count on to support you through prayer and encouragement during this challenging time.

Meditation

In the initial days, weeks, and months that follow catastrophic loss, pain reigns supreme; this is a normal and necessary passage. In our own time, however, we will gather strength to forge a new tomorrow. There is great power in our ability to choose our own path. We can be held captive by no dilemma or person, no sorrow or grave, no deprivation or attitude. We are completely free to choose our response to even the most horrific of life's dark circumstances. We possess the freedom to celebrate life in a way that reflects joy rather than resentment, gratitude rather than self-pity. We by no means escape tragedy's deep sorrow, but up from the ashes, in its own season, a delicate yet vibrant flower will grow.

> Be anxious for nothing, but in everything by prayer and supplication with thanksgiving let your requests be made known to God. And the peace of God, which surpasses all comprehension, will guard your hearts and your minds in Christ Jesus. (PHILIPPIANS 4:6-7)

Summary

Previous illusions of safety long since gone, we have learned that catastrophic loss chooses its own means and timing to snatch away our sense of security and peace. The cascade of loss that typically follows our initial misfortune can engender feelings of despair and hopelessness, and we struggle just to maintain our balance in what now seems to be a chaotic world.

Despite the turmoil that stirs up our fears, we possess the ability to come face to face with loss. Grief never offers us a round-trip ticket to the same world that we enjoyed prior to our loss; and it rarely, if ever, gives us a smooth ride to our next destination. We can, however, prepare ourselves for the uncharted journey. Not only is there an empathetic community of others ready to support us, there are also seeds of resiliency deep within us waiting to be cultivated. As we gather our resources, we can call upon God to provide us with strength and courage for what lies ahead.

In working through this chapter, consider the ways you have grown. What have you learned about yourself and about your loss?

RECOMMENDED READING

Chapters 1 and 2 of *A Grace Disguised,* by Gerald Sittser

Chapter 1 of *How Can It Be All Right When Everything Is All Wrong?* by Lewis B. Smedes

Part 1 of *The Courage to Grieve,* by Judy Tatelbaum

The Reluctant Traveler

Our Initial Response to Loss

Blessed be the LORD,
who daily bears our burden.
(PSALM 68:19)

The Uninvited Guest

We humans are creatures of habit. We bask in the reflection of set patterns of living and soak up the rays of predictability that tell us all is well with our world. Belief in our ability to control life and its circumstances lulls us into a false sense of security when all appears to be in its proper place. With the illusion of being "in charge," we go about our daily life as though impervious to harm, certain that bad things happen only to "other people." When unsolicited change does knock at our door, we are hesitant to invite it in to enjoy the warmth of a life carefully arranged. Instead, change is often turned away, left on the cold doorstep without a second glance from us. But what about the kind of change that refuses to be ignored?

Catastrophic loss is not known for its good manners, or its deference for protocol or patience. Rather than knock politely at our front door, loss audaciously enters without permission. At times it may boldly barge into our life, such as when we unexpectedly lose a loved one or have a serious accident. Or it can surreptitiously slink in through a side window, as when a significant relationship slowly deteriorates or a chronic illness claims a life by bits and pieces. The jolt that accompanies initial awareness of this type of loss sends messages of urgency throughout body and mind, warning us of the impending danger of unwanted change. A reflexive cry of protest expresses itself in an outpouring of emotion. Life as we know it is ripped from our grasp, forcing us to become a reluctant traveler in unfamiliar and frightening territory, with the safe comfort of home seeming only a faraway memory.

Disbelief, fear, anxiety, and confusion begin to overwhelm our capacity to cope effectively with the onslaught of unsolicited change. Soon a state of bewilderment sets in like a heavy, damp fog, restricting visibility. Our attempts to gain a clear understanding of circumstances are impeded by a dizzying array of questions. *How did this happen? Whose fault is it? What will I do now? How can I ever be the same? Is life even worth living? Can't I just forget this and go back to the way things were?* With our mind in overdrive and our body on a constant state of alert, we run the risk of depleting our limited resources. Eventually we sink into a state of numbness, as circumstances take on a surreal quality and our feelings become curiously bland. It is at this point that self-doubt creeps in.

Defending Against Devastation

> Some of our pain is shut off, as if we are partially anesthetized. Experiences are blurred or hazy. We seem to be living as if in a dream.[1] JUDY TATELBAUM

People experiencing a state of detachment may occasionally feel uncomfortable with their lack of connection to the world around them. They may question whether or not they really care about the people and circumstances surrounding their losses; they may even begin to worry that something is terribly wrong with them. To the contrary, psychologists believe this "disconnect" is a normal and essential part of the grieving process that lends itself to the increased probability of healthy resolution. With the threat of devastation hovering over like a dark cloud, detachment allows us the emotional distance we need to gather the strength and resources necessary to go forward with life. Some typical indicators of this phase of grieving include the following:

A feeling of numbness	Experiencing life as surreal
A desire to give up	Feelings of helplessness
Disbelief	Lack of concern
Inability to access feelings	Refusal to acknowledge circumstances
Inability to cry	Unwillingness to discuss the loss

Describe any indicators you are aware of that reflect your experience with detachment.

Reflect on your feelings and concerns about the experience of detachment.

Some of the behaviors that emerge to ward off the sense of impending doom connected to catastrophic loss are what psychologists call ego defense mechanisms. According to experts, although defense mechanisms can assume different forms, they are quite normal and serve the same purpose of cushioning the blow of difficult circumstances. Furthermore, it is believed that the selection of behavior happens, for the most part, at an unconscious level, and is influenced by our developmental stage (child, adolescent, adult) and the degree of anxiety (mild, moderate, severe) we are experiencing as a result of loss.

Following are several mechanisms that typically appear in the initial stage of loss, along with examples of how the defense might appear to an observer.

Repression: Memories of a traumatic event are sealed off from conscious thought.

An incest victim removes the horrific circumstances of her life from conscious memory in order to continue functioning as if "all is well" in her world. She may compensate for the lack of control in her personal life by becoming an overachiever at school or work.

Rationalization: An attempt is made to explain away disappointments or defend behavior.

> Having lost his job because of poor performance, the ex-employee manages his anxiety by convincing himself and others that the job was of a caliber well below his abilities and talents. He blames his occupational woes on boredom and a boss unable to recognize his promising potential.

Denial: Aspects of reality that are unpleasant or painful are ignored. Unlike other defense mechanisms, this typically occurs on the subconscious or conscious level rather than the unconscious level.

> Hoping against hope, a young husband and father denies the seriousness of his wife's mental illness, insisting that family members not mention their concerns. His children are not allowed to directly speak about Mommy's withdrawn and sometimes frightening behavior.

Regression: Effort is made to rely on behaviors that were once outgrown.

> After the shock of discovering her husband's unfaithfulness, a woman attempts to comfort herself with favorite childhood foods even though her diabetes precludes their consumption.

Reflect on your observations of significant people in your life who have experienced loss. Describe the defense mechanisms they used to initially cope with challenges.

Of the four major types of defense mechanisms used in the early stages of grieving, which two do you feel you relied on the most? Describe your uses of these and how they helped you to cope.

> I had to plan memorial services. I also had to take care of my two older children, who were terrified and confused by the accident, having been pushed, as it were, out of their cozy home and into a blizzard of pain. During those first busy days, however, I was rational enough to know that darkness loomed ahead and that I would soon descend into it.[2] GERALD SITTSER

Ego defense mechanisms allow us to take in the true meaning of loss at our own pace. They may also provide the gift of time to attend to the immediate business of post-loss survival without the additional burden of emotional turmoil. For example:

> After losing her home in a tragic fire, a woman is able to provide information to the fire department and her insurance agent, arrange for her children to stay with relatives, and find homes willing to temporarily provide care for the family's pets. It is only after the majority of details are attended to that the deep anguish begins to surface as she recalls the loss of precious and irreplaceable mementos consumed by the fire, significant reminders of a cherished past gone forever.

List examples of the loss-related tasks you were able to accomplish during the time that defense mechanisms caused you to detach.

Describe the feelings that surfaced as the initial wave of post-loss survival business ebbed.

Open your sketchbook to a blank page. With your eyes closed, draw a picture that reflects your total experience of detachment at this early stage of grieving.

Taking a Wrong Turn

Defense mechanisms are neither all good nor all bad. In this respect they are very much like our feelings. The fact that we experience anger, for example, is not in and of itself problematic. The real issue is how we choose to use our anger. When we use anger to fuel constructive change in our life, its influence is positive. However, when we allow our feelings to rage out of control, hurting others and creating problems for ourselves, anger is no longer our friend. The same holds true for defense mechanisms. Just as denial or rationalization can help us cope during stress-filled times, they can also turn on us, refusing to part company when their usefulness has faded. When this happens, they cause our undoing.

What are the signs that indicate our defense mechanisms have gone too far or out-lived their usefulness? And what can we do if we see those signs? Given the uniqueness of each individual, the answers to these challenging questions can prove elusive. In general, avoiding or altering reality should never become a preferred lifestyle, but this does not mean that we should immediately jump into the thick of things, trying to iron out life's every wrinkle. What it does mean is that we can expect, after a reasonable passage of time, to begin facing up to both difficult feelings and burdensome challenges created by our loss.

Although defense mechanisms are born in the unconscious, their expression becomes tangible and concrete as they are played out in our behavior. Here are some examples of behaviors that have reached the unhealthy stage:

- ▶ A continued sense of detachment that negatively impacts personal or professional relationships
- ▶ Lingering feelings of numbness interrupted by periodic bouts of intense anxiety

▶ Exacerbation of previous physical ailments or the emergence of new ones that seem resistant to healing
▶ Actions that cause repeated expressions of concern by family or friends
▶ Extreme and persistent fatigue
▶ Ongoing, intractable confusion
▶ Continued withdrawal from previously enjoyed activities
▶ Emergence or exacerbation of addictive behaviors

Reflect on a time when you were concerned about someone close to you who seemed stuck in the mire of detachment following a loss. Describe what that looked like.

Have you, or someone close to you, identified any behaviors that may indicate that you are struggling with a prolonged state of detachment following your loss? If so, describe the observable behaviors that are of concern.

Many of us who find ourselves "stuck" in a state of detachment fear we will never again "feel" to the same degree that we did prior to our loss. The deadness we experience seems intractable, oppressive, permanent. We must, however, take into account the magnitude of the trauma and the cascade of loss it generated. If we judge the loss to be greater than we feel equipped to handle, then prolonged detachment seems like a normal response to an abnormal situation. The important thing to remember at this point is that we are not alone. Many people who have found themselves stuck in the detachment phase have managed to get "unstuck" with the support of family and friends, and/or the assistance of a licensed professional counselor or psychologist.

Describe your fear of "getting stuck" and the reasons why you feel you are not equipped to deal with the loss.

Using the lens of logic, how reasonable do you think your feelings and beliefs are about your ability to deal with loss?

Now go back to chapter 1 to review your list of resiliency traits and the plan you developed to cultivate a new trait. Write about the progress you have made in realizing the fruits of your plan.

What other action do you wish to take to further your growth and help you to get "unstuck"? Consider talking with someone you know who has also experienced a loss.

Packing for the Journey

> We are here to be changed, to be made more like God in order to prepare us for a lifetime with him. And that process may be served by the mysterious pattern of all creation; pleasure sometimes emerges against a background of pain, evil may be transformed into good, and suffering may produce something of value.[3] PHILIP YANCEY

As the state of detachment begins to fade, we have an opportunity to prepare for our unique journey through grief. Because each loss is distinct, with its own set of circumstances and needs, the act of equipping ourselves must be approached as though it is recovery's maiden voyage. It is difficult to imagine such preparation, given that we instinctively resist pain. An innate fear of an unknown future causes most of us to drag our feet when it comes to pulling out the suitcase. Why would we pack for a trip we neither planned nor want to take? But because we don't have the option of canceling, just how can we brace ourselves for such a dark excursion?

Perhaps among the most helpful preparatory strategies is education. Educating ourselves about the grieving process improves our resiliency. Information illuminates the darkness and allows us to make sense of our loss in light of the experience of others. Knowing that fellow travelers faced with similar difficulties not only survived but grew from their experiences provides us with a much-needed model of hope. Being realistic yet optimistic loosens loss's powerful grip on our life.

What have you learned about loss from the recommended readings?

Beyond education, we can prepare ourselves for what lies ahead by exploring the potential impact of loss with regard to short-term and long-term consequences that will require our response. For example, following the trauma of a physical assault and mugging, a person is faced with a number of challenges. Consider these possibilities.

Immediate:

- ▶ Get needed medical attention
- ▶ Contact police to report the crime
- ▶ Share experience with family members
- ▶ Contact credit card companies to cancel stolen cards and request new ones
- ▶ Contact the Department of Motor Vehicles to apply for a new license

More long-term:

- ▶ Work with the medical insurance company to pay medical bills
- ▶ Reformat monthly budget to compensate for money stolen during the mugging, and for lost wages during recuperation

▶ Plan for a safer route home from work

▶ Identify a fellow worker to commute with

▶ Rearrange schedule to go to physical therapy appointments and follow-up visits with the physician

▶ Together with family members, identify therapeutic support to work through issues of fear and anger

List the immediate repercussions of your loss.

What are some of the more long-term repercussions of your loss?

As we survey all that encompasses our loss it is important to be patient with ourselves and the grieving process. In doing so, we will be better able to manage the stress and sorrow that lie ahead. It is likely that we will be called to new responsibilities as we attempt to navigate various aspects of our journey. Knowing what to expect allows us the opportunity to reach beyond a mere reflexive response to summon the assets and resources we possess. Assets to consider include:

▶ Personal resiliency traits

▶ Personal gifts and talents

▶ Social support system

▶ Community resources

▶ Financial resources

To return to our example, the person who was mugged might pause to reflect on assets and resources that will help him through his ordeal. His list might look like this:

- ▶ Personal resiliency traits—My belief that any negative situation can be used for positive growth
- ▶ Personal gifts and talents—Positive attitude, creative, determined
- ▶ Social support system—My spouse, my two children, my sister, and my two best friends
- ▶ Community resources—Support group for victims of violent crime, supportive church family
- ▶ Financial resources—Enough in savings to cover the first two months of bills while being out of work

Considering the major categories, make a list of assets and resources available to you.

Personal resiliency traits:

Personal gifts and talents:

Social support system:

Community resources:

Financial resources:

Which area(s) would you like to further cultivate to support yourself in the grief process?

One final area of preparation focuses on the reactions of others as they learn about our loss. Each of us is immersed in various "sub-communities" that may include immediate family, extended family, friends, neighbors, church family, fellow employees, and the general community in which we live. With this multiple membership status comes the reality that we may be called to process a number of different reactions depending upon who is aware of our loss and how they perceive it. Loss can be public or private, is considered acceptable or unacceptable, and brings with it an increase or decrease in status.

Categorical Examples of Loss

Public Loss	**Private Loss**
Death	Miscarriage
Divorce	Sexual abuse
Natural disaster	Loss of a dream
Loss of job	Illness

For example, contrast a private loss (illness), viewed as acceptable (hereditary condition), that increases our status (we are considered courageous for living with the pain) with a public loss (divorce), viewed as unacceptable (unsanctioned by the religious community), that results in a loss of status (social stigma). The reactions of others will be colored by the culture in which they are immersed, their relationships with us (or lack thereof), their values and beliefs, and their life experiences. Given all the possible permutations to this complex formula, preparing for these reactions can be a daunting task at best. We can, however, separate ourselves and our self-worth from the opinion of others by simply attempting to understand their point of view.

Regardless of whether or not we feel generously supported or unfairly judged, we honor others by allowing them the freedom to express their viewpoints. In so doing, we stretch our own boundaries for empathy and compassion when we see others hurting.

How do you believe your loss is viewed by others? Is it considered public or private? Acceptable or unacceptable? Does it increase or decrease your status?

What are your thoughts and feelings about how others view your loss?

How can you use this part of your loss experience for growth?

Spiritual Reflection

> Faith does not break loose in my head with a whooping, "Hurrah for God!"
> Believing sneaks into my soul while my mind is saying, "My God, where were
> you when I needed you?"[4] LEWIS SMEDES

The phone call came at dusk, at the end of a busy November weekday, in the midst of
the usual happy chaos so typical of our family's after-school activities. The businesslike
voice penetrating the receiver informed me of a pending crisis that would ultimately
plunge my family into the depths of raw fear and despair. As I placed the phone back
in its cradle I felt the first wave of shock. After undergoing a biopsy, my brother,
Michael, learned that he was about to engage in a battle for his life. How could this be?
He was too young and too vibrant to have cancer invade and destroy his happiness. I
was the one who usually wrestled with health challenges; why hadn't I contracted the
disease instead?

I promised Michael that night that I would begin praying not only for his healing,
but also for wisdom and guidance for his medical team, and courage for the journey.
He politely informed me that given his lack of belief, he saw no possibility of fruit being
realized from such an exercise. I assured him that healing was not contingent upon his
belief; God blesses believers as well as those who fancy themselves skeptics. I boldly
proclaimed proof of this truth in the fact that the splendor of nature was available for
all to enjoy, regardless of their spiritual inclinations. Faithfully, day after day for the next
five months, despite evidence to the contrary, I prayed that my brother be granted a
miraculous recovery. It was not until the moment an emergency-room physician
informed us that Michael had mere hours left to live that I ceased my hope-filled peti-
tions and instead prayed for a merciful ending to his agony.

Three days following my brother's death, without the gift of time to work through
my feelings and find answers to difficult spiritual questions, I was faced with another
emerging crisis: my father's illness. As its seriousness became more apparent, I suddenly found myself engulfed in a stormy struggle to pray for yet another miraculous
healing. I was able to pray for the strength and courage to face this new challenge; I
was even able to ask God to guide the physicians who attended to my father's wel-
fare; but try as I might, I could not find it within me to implore God to bless my father
with restored health. Like a boat mercilessly tossed about in an unexpected squall, I
lost my balance in the tumultuous waves of doubt and despair. Spiritual vertigo hit me
full-force like a great gust of wind, coming out of nowhere and leaving me dizzy with
apprehension. The shock of loss that accompanied my brother's passing cast an omi-
nous shadow over my previous belief in divine intervention. *Why had God allowed
Michael to die? Where was God when I needed Him? Did my voice no longer summon
His attention? Why did He allow death to so quickly stalk yet another of my loved ones?*

For the first time ever in my walk of faith, a queasy feeling of dread and uncertainty threatened to submerge my soul.

In the ensuing months, despite my doubts, I tenaciously clung to God for survival. Deep within me, in my heart of hearts, I knew that God would patiently instruct me in His ways. I was sure of the fierce love He possessed for His children, a love that would not allow abandonment, even in light of my new spiritual insecurities and questions. My confidence in Him grew as I was reminded of the pain and suffering He experienced in His desire to restore us to Himself. Weary from grief's pain, I chose to rest in God's arms like a small child, trusting that divine wisdom superseded what my human eyes judged to be senseless. Perhaps someday I would understand, but for today I would simply leave my questions at the foot of the cross.

List the difficult spiritual questions you have wrestled with in the midst of your loss.

Describe some of the feelings that emerged as a result of the questions you listed.

In your sketchbook, using your nondominant hand, draw a picture that represents the spiritual vertigo you have experienced.

For this turbulent time in your spiritual life, record truths that support trust in God. You may want to use such inspirational sources as songs, hymns, meditation books, or the Bible.

List two people whom you feel will be helpful as you sort through challenging spiritual questions.

Make a commitment to contact one of the people listed. Find a mutually agreeable time for an in-depth discussion.

▶ Meditation

When the way is dark with life's challenges, and we are unsure of how to navigate to safety, fear and confusion become constant traveling companions. It is during these times that God teaches us to look to Him for direction. With our assent, the Divine Navigator steers us to a place of rest where strength is renewed and joy's promise returns.

No longer the reluctant traveler,
No longer frightened by the foe,
No need to journey in the dark,
No need to be alone.[5]
DIANE DEMPSEY MARR

Summary

In the initial hours and days following the realization of catastrophic loss, our body and mind find a means to protect us from the full force of its impact. During this phase, when feelings are numbed, we have the opportunity to prepare for a time when the veil of protection will slowly be lifted and the true meaning of loss will be realized. Taking good care of ourselves physically, mentally, and spiritually will be important in the days ahead. Preparing for the challenges is made easier as we review the personal assets and resources available to us. In addition, we can explore difficult spiritual questions as we seek to understand the meaning of our experiences with the darker side of life.

In working through this chapter, what have you learned about yourself and your loss?

In your sketchbook, create a collage that captures these thoughts and feelings.

Consult chapter 8 if you want to learn more about developing a plan for self-care.

RECOMMENDED READING

Chapters 3 and 4 of *A Grace Disguised,* by Gerald Sittser

Chapters 3 and 4 of *The Courage to Grieve,* by Judy Tatelbaum

Parts 1 and 2 of *Where Is God When It Hurts?* by Philip Yancey

Grim Night's Verdict

The Realization That We Are Forever Changed

Surely our griefs He Himself bore,
And our sorrows He carried.
(ISAIAH 53:4)

Fury's Unknown Destination

As the fog of detachment slowly burns away, reality, once obscured by the murky gray vapor, comes to the forefront of our realization. Unveiling the previously unfathomable devastation created by catastrophic loss, we are no longer protected by the numbing state of denial. It is at this place—the very underbelly of raw pain—that we must confront our forever-altered existence while the rest of the world blithely goes about the business of daily living. A husband rolls to the empty side of the bed only to realize he will never again share it with the wife he loved. A mother faces the arduous task of caring for a chronically ill child who once thrived. A man awakes promptly at 6 A.M. only to remember that there is nowhere to go since he lost his job. The triggers that bring forth the pain of loss highlight the unfairness of misfortune. Like the blazing heat of a summer's afternoon, this newfound sensitivity ignites a deep anger within us that is not easily extinguished.

Fanning the flames of this growing anger are our many expectations and beliefs that have somehow proven themselves inadequate or false. Loss violently shakes the world on which we once confidently stood, bringing into question our most foundational convictions. Cherishing the institution of marriage and its vow of monogamy does not guarantee that a spouse will not choose to give his or her heart to another. Valuing consistent and responsible behavior does not prevent job loss. The capricious shifting sands of human existence wear away at our self-confidence and faith. Catapulting us directly into the waiting arms of fear turned to anger, the gale force winds of happenstance make evident our lack of control. Beliefs about how the world should function cast a feeble light on the reality we now experience.

Our anger is further kindled by the cascade of loss likely to follow our initial loss. We have barely recognized and absorbed the meaning of our primary loss when we are overtaken by the immensity of greater destruction. *Haven't we suffered enough?* Weary from the battle, we sink deeper into the mire, feeling victimized by the unfairness of our situation. Flown as a banner above our head, outrage and indignation announce our despair to any who would attempt to support us during these tumultuous times.

As a final blow, we discover that not all onlookers are understanding or comfortable with our pain. Protecting themselves against the fear of a similar fate, they project their anxiety through the cold, discerning eye of logic.

I distinctly remember my shock upon hearing one friend's comments following the death of my father. Without hesitation he announced that this was an example of the inevitable circle of nature and, given my life stage, I should get used to it. Besides, he reasoned, I should view such occurrences positively, because they would make me a more compassionate human being. Though both comments possess an element of truth, applicable to a variety of losses, they do not come close to what a grieving person longs to hear. At the very least, these distancing devices—making insensitive comments, ignoring another's loss, or abruptly ending conversations with the promise to pray—leave their recipient lonely and isolated. Most certainly they provide ample fuel to continue feeding the fire of misfortune's anger.

Sadly, given most people's uneasiness with our anger, it seems easiest just to mask it. But anger cannot be ignored, for its potential to become an obstacle to resolving grief is real. Despite the fact that some people seem comfortable using anger as a blanket of protection, most of us grow increasingly uncomfortable when entrenched in this volatile and energy-draining emotional state. This is not to say that we should distance ourselves from anger as quickly as it appears in our rearview mirror. Anger, in and of itself, is not necessarily bad. If we are able to harness its energy properly, anger can swiftly lead us to creative solutions to some of life's most challenging problems. However, if anger overtakes us on the road to finding a solution, we may lose our ability to make sound choices as we speed toward fury's unknown destination. It seems important then to educate ourselves about all aspects of grief's wrath so we can decide who will be in the driver's seat, rather than allowing anger to make the decision for us.

Defining Anger

Anger is a natural reaction to loss's unplanned and unwanted change. This change typically remains outside of our control, leaving us in an agitated state marked by feelings of helplessness and fear. The *American Heritage Dictionary* defines *anger* in the following manner:

> a strong feeling of displeasure and belligerence.[1]

Consider the following responses to loss that expose deep disappointment and the presence of anger:

- ▶ I will never be the same.
- ▶ I did not choose this.
- ▶ It's not fair!
- ▶ Despite all of my efforts, this happened anyway.
- ▶ I don't deserve this.
- ▶ People will always look at me differently now.
- ▶ Why can't this be somebody else's problem?
- ▶ How can anybody get over something like this?
- ▶ I feel like damaged goods.
- ▶ This seems absolutely senseless.
- ▶ Why me? Why my family?

Describe some initial thoughts you had about your loss that reveal feelings of anger and disappointment.

Anger's Relatives: *Resentment, Bitterness,* and *Rage*

Most of us recoil at the sight of these words because they symbolize a major source of pain and devastation for humans across all cultures. To think that they have somehow weaseled their way into our life is more than we can bear. How did this happen? How does the normal experience of anger go astray? Before these questions are answered, we need to define the terms for anger's three closest relatives.

> *resentment:* to feel or show displeasure or indignation.
> *bitterness:* characterized by intense hostility or resentment.
> *rage:* violent anger or fury.[2]

Anger and its relatives can best be understood by using the metaphor of a tree. *Anger* is the seedling that springs forth spontaneously when the ground is fertilized by loss. If the seedling is supplied with ample water, its roots will grow deeper as it reaches toward its own burning sun. This is where *resentment* enters in. Springing from our original anger, resentment sprouts its new shoots as we begin to ruminate about the unfairness and pain of our loss. Issues seem to grow with each passing day as we wrestle with negative feelings. Unable to resolve our anger, we unwittingly fertilize this new growth, allowing it to mature into a sturdy, well-nourished sapling. It is at this point that most of us grow weary of tending to our anger. With less water and sunlight, though, resentment withers and anger fades as we learn to resolve our issues.

Describe any resentment you have experienced as a result of grief's pain.

Occasionally we can be so wounded that we are unable to manage the pain that accompanies loss. Resentment continues to nurture the sapling, eventually transforming it into a mature tree. It is here that *bitterness* enters the scene. Like the maggot that attacks weakened trees, bitterness worms its way into the very core of our being and becomes firmly rooted in our heart. Anchored securely by ever-growing anger, bitterness drains its host of emotional well-being and spiritual vitality. In our fragile state, it is difficult to find the energy needed to purge ourselves of this life-draining pest.

If bitterness has overtaken you as a result of your loss, explain its impact on your life and your relationships with others.

If left unchecked, bitterness can give birth to a more formidable foe: *rage*. Rage is an opportunistic predator. It takes advantage of the barren landscape created by bitterness and feeds on the spoils of anger. Rage is hurt magnified, pain amplified, and anger out of control. Like unpredictable wildfire, it blinds us to reality, robs us of the opportunity to problem-solve, does our thinking for us, and ultimately chooses our behavior. Without the aid of logic, common sense, or higher-order values, rage determines a source for its pain, projecting responsibility for our loss onto any number of sources: the government, big business, a professional group, coworkers, friends, family—even God Himself. Lacking interest in the accuracy of choice, rage blazes ahead, consuming its prey. When rage has finally spent itself, we wake up to the nightmare of smoking devastation it has left in its wake.

Have you experienced any thoughts or behaviors that might indicate that rage is, or could become, a problem?

In your sketchbook, draw a picture or create a collage that represents your loss and the subsequent experience with anger and its relatives.

Anger's Murky Waters

> Be angry, and yet do not sin; do not let the sun go down on your anger, and do not give the devil an opportunity. (EPHESIANS 4:26-27)

People who cling to anger inevitably find themselves in a wrestling match with at least one of anger's relatives. Whether resentment, bitterness, or rage, each is a formidable opponent to grief recovery in its own right. They whisper to our imagination, convincing us that we are justified in nursing our anger, given our new victim status. They patiently wait for our weakest moments, when hunger, fatigue, or stress gets the best of us, before launching their attacks. They cleverly hide just below the surface of our consciousness so as not to draw attention to themselves, but can surface swiftly when provoked. They cause us to read the intentions of others in a negative way, preparing us to expect aggression and hostility from even our most treasured relationships.

When we buy into their rationalizations, anger's relatives gladly take charge of our world. Slowly and surely they rob us of our flexibility, tolerance, and trust. Our once cherished relationships collapse under the weight of this magnified anger, leaving us with isolation and depression as our only willing companions. Peace becomes a rare commodity.

If you have struggled with overly aggressive expressions of anger or rage, describe the difficulties they have caused you and others.

Those of us on the "receiving end" have often been traumatized by our interactions with these prisoners of anger. We know what it's like to be the target of another's rage or to feel the hopelessness of trying to break through an impenetrable fortress of bitterness. Influenced by these negative experiences, we either pretend we are not angry or turn our anger inward when it is our turn to deal with loss. However, whether we choose to deny anger's existence or elect to punish ourselves, we lose touch with our true selves by trading interpersonal peace for such difficulties as chronic depression, anxiety, guilt, or shame.

In light of our discomfort with this feeling state, it is not surprising that society applauds our ability to swallow anger. Despite the violence portrayed in the popular media, society continues to frown on the expression of anger. Many of us grew up in families in which we were not allowed any expression of anger. Yet frequently, behind closed doors, we were targets for adult tempers. In the absence of healthy models, we lack the tools to effectively deal with our anger and express it appropriately. And the toll it takes on our relationships, as well as our physical and mental health, is difficult to ignore.

Make a list of messages from society or your family that get in the way of identifying or admitting the anger connected to your loss.

Describe some of the physical symptoms or mental challenges you have experienced as a result of allowing anger to overpower your life.

Loosening Anger's Grip

> Since pain is a part of every person's experience, we would do well to learn how to deal with this emotional gargoyle.[3] RUTH STAPLETON

Loosening anger's grip on our lives may be the most daunting task we face in the grieving process. As we have seen, anger and its relatives have the uncanny ability to snatch away life's joy, leaving us drained and despondent with little hope for a brighter future. This is, without a doubt, the bad news. The good news is that we have an opportunity to harness anger's energy to power a fuller life; one filled with a keener sense of enjoyment, compassion, and tranquility. In this sense anger becomes a protective factor, one which fuels our personal growth.

Intimately familiar with catastrophic loss, renowned psychiatrist Viktor Frankl believed that people could harness their energies to transform even the bleakest of circumstances. According to his teachings, this is more than a remote possibility. The one simple factor that opens up this possibility is our refusal to assume the role of victim. Frankl himself survived the German concentration camps of World War II, only to discover that his wife and family had perished at the hands of the Nazis. Despite this devastating blow, Frankl, determined to live life to its fullest, refused to be held prisoner by his past. He went on to once again experience the love of a family and to become one of the twentieth century's most powerful influences in the field of psychology. Frankl's story is a testament to the resiliency of the human spirit.

As was the case with Viktor Frankl, we too have both the freedom and the responsibility to choose our attitude about the hand that life has dealt us. Even in the face of catastrophic loss, we can actively choose to make peace with our anger, and in the process, free up precious emotional energy needed to recover from grief's sting. Instead of allowing challenges to paralyze our desire to live courageously, we can choose to empower ourselves with the knowledge that significant life-transforming meaning can be born out of any and all circumstances. How do we get to the point where we are ready to move beyond our anger, and what does this process entail? To resolve anger, we must be willing to walk through the following five steps:

1. Admit that anger is present.
2. Identify the source of the anger.
3. Explore anger's many facets.
4. Identify a means of releasing the anger.
5. Become willing to let go of the anger.

Describe some of your reactions to the anger resolution process.

At this point in your recovery, how ready do you feel to walk through the process?

What would help you to become more fully prepared?

List the resiliency factors that you already possess to help you navigate the anger resolution process. (For a list of factors, consult page 24.)

The Anger Resolution Process

STEP ONE: ADMIT THAT ANGER IS PRESENT.

Preparing ourselves to work through the anger resolution process means "stepping up to the plate" and admitting our anger. Any number of things can keep us from such an admission. We may struggle with how we will be perceived by others. We may hesitate because we believe our anger is justified and does not require removal. Perhaps the party responsible for our pain has yet to own his or her part in our suffering. Letting go of our anger might mean letting that person off the hook. Regardless of circumstances, anger eventually transforms itself from a positive, protective emotion to an energy-sapping burden. Admitting our anger is the first step in letting go of that load weighing us down.

Discuss any personal challenges that might keep you from admitting your anger.

In the previous section, you listed messages from society and family that had the potential to prevent you from identifying your anger. Putting the influence of such edicts aside, describe your feelings as you freely admit your anger.

STEP TWO: IDENTIFY THE SOURCE OF THE ANGER.

With the admission of anger, we are now free to take a closer look at the source of that anger. Reflecting on our total experience with loss highlights different aspects of it that we find troubling. Many times the cascade of loss that follows our initial loss creates a deluge of anger issues. This concept is illustrated in the following example.

A thirty-something mother sought counseling to deal with issues of unresolved anger. Her chief complaint was that of depression and an inability to enjoy her family. In recalling her childhood and the early and unexpected death of her mother, the woman explored the extent of her loss and its impact on her life. By doing so, she was able to identify the following anger issues that needed to be put to rest:

▶ She was angry with her mother for dying and leaving her alone with a father who had never shown interest in her or her siblings. She was lonely and afraid.
▶ She was angry with God for allowing the birth of her baby sister to ultimately put an end to her mother's life. This was not fair to her or to her baby sister.
▶ She was angry with her brother for always creating more problems for the family. Because of him, her father never had any time for the rest of the children.
▶ She was angry with her older sister for leaving the responsibility of taking care of the baby to her. She had to grow up too soon.
▶ It was hard for her to accept that the doctors seemed uninterested in making her mother comfortable during the last few days of her final illness. It was difficult to see her mother in so much pain.
▶ She was angry because her children would never know their grandmother.

By identifying sources of anger connected to our loss we create an important blueprint that helps us to understand our experience. If we are to rebuild our lives, then we must focus on issues that need to be resolved.

Identify the various sources of your anger and list them below.

STEP THREE: EXPLORE ANGER'S MANY FACETS.

Many people feel overwhelmed by the thought of attempting to resolve their anger, particularly in light of the many aspects of life with which anger can become entangled. Let's return to the previous illustration involving the young mother. As we review her list of unresolved anger issues from childhood, we can guess the types of issues she may be struggling with today.

- ▶ She may fear abandonment, given her mother's early death.
- ▶ She may view men as emotionally distant and difficult to please.
- ▶ She may struggle with her spirituality.
- ▶ She may be overly responsible, having little sense of relaxation or playfulness.
- ▶ She is likely to have little faith in the medical profession.

Our baggage from the past can easily become attached to the present challenges, thereby complicating our experience of anger. Exploring the many facets of our anger allows us to uncover these complications, separate the past from the present, and begin working toward resolution of each issue.

Record any past history that may be adding to the complexity of your anger today.

STEP FOUR: IDENTIFY A MEANS OF RELEASING THE ANGER.

Beyond exploring the dimensions of our anger on a cognitive level as we did in Steps Two and Three, we must give anger a voice to enable the release of related emotions. By doing so, we externalize our anger, bringing it outside of ourselves in preparation for its final release. The way in which we choose to articulate anger's emotions will depend on:

- ▶ the type of loss we have experienced,
- ▶ the belief we have in our ability to manage strong emotions, and
- ▶ the creativity we bring to the process.

Because each of us represents a unique set of needs, the process will look quite different from person to person. Regardless of our chosen approach, the avenue we pursue for anger's release must be one that encourages full expression of the depth of our pain. The following story illustrates these concepts.

A teenage cancer survivor struggled for some time with conflicted feelings. On the one hand, she was grateful for her experience, as it had cemented in her mind the preciousness of ordinary life and the gifts of friends and family. Her battle, however, also gave birth to an anger she had not previously encountered. Naive no more, the fragility of life had become a stark reality. Emerging from the backdrop of cancer's invasive reach, she felt cheated out of her birthright and robbed of her youth. She grieved the loss of her dream—her desire for the perfect family, of children that would never be. She lamented the fact that she could no longer experience life as her friends did. Youth unaware, they challenged death at every turn, driving carelessly, experimenting with drugs, and playing roulette with their sexualities. Even though she found none of these behaviors attractive, she simply longed for the return to an innocent state that protected her from death's cold grip and the reality of broken dreams.

This young woman instinctively knew that dwelling on things forever lost would rob her of her ability to celebrate what was left of her youth. Not wanting to sink deeper into anger's quicksand, she became determined to release her negative feelings. After much thought, she fashioned a unique means of accomplishing this task. On small slips of paper she wrote down every facet of her anger of which she was aware. She rolled these slips up tightly and inserted them into a bouquet of balloons and had the balloons filled with helium. The young woman then took the balloons to the top of an isolated, grassy knoll and released each balloon separately while yelling out specific reasons for her anger. Molded to her particular needs, it was this vocalization of pain (and the noisy send-off) that allowed her to go forward with the healing process.

Following are some additional examples of both symbolic and actual means people have used to assist in the process of releasing their anger.

Symbolic Avenues of Release:

Engaging in a symbolic dialogue with anger
Journaling
Placing symbols of anger in a box and later burying it
Throwing rocks into a river or ocean while verbalizing anger

Unraveling audio tapes as a means of destroying "old tapes" from the
   past
Writing a letter that is never sent and later disposing of it in some type
   of ceremony (burning it in the fireplace, ripping it to shreds and
   throwing them into the wind)

Actual Avenues of Release:

Making a genuine attempt at forgiveness
Sending a carefully written letter that allows the recipient to understand
   the impact his or her behavior had on you
Sharing a poem, picture, or song that reflects your feelings
With the assistance of a counselor, confronting the person who hurt you

What are some concerns you have about your ability to manage strong emotions?

Use your creativity to brainstorm some safe and effective ways to release your anger and pain.

Which alternatives make the most sense in light of your concerns about managing strong emotions?

Reflect on your need for support during the anger resolution process, and the type of assistance you will seek.

STEP FIVE: Become willing to let go of the anger.

If we were to conduct a survey, I think most of us would agree that anger is not an emotion we want to keep around for any length of time. Hanging on to anger is like walking through life carrying a backpack full of an ever-growing collection of heavy rocks. Nobody would argue the fact that they are "our rocks." We earned them through daily interaction with a sometimes insensitive and callous world. But let's be honest—after a while, hauling around all those rocks gets downright old. Soon we may forget how those rocks got into our backpack in the first place! All we know is that, because of the weight of the rocks, our shoulders are aching and our energy is sapped. We are no longer sure we want to dedicate our limited resources to hauling the rocks around with us.

Hanging on to past anger is not only burdensome and exhausting, it is unhealthy as well. Creating a plethora of problems that could have been avoided, the person who insists on hoarding anger and pain slowly trains his or her powers of observation on the negative rather than the positive aspects of everything. Over time, this negative bent robs us of our ability to appreciate and enjoy life. Soon we subconsciously define existence as a series of events to survive rather than the unfolding of daily miracles.

The simple solution to this dilemma, of course, is to let go of our anger. The anger resolution process is just that—a process. It would be most advantageous if we could simply follow a convenient linear model whose final step signaled a nice, neat completion to a job well done. However, just like the rest of life, working through anger can be messy. It takes time, patience, and the understanding that we may be required to fall back to previous steps when new issues come to our awareness. Accepting this fact allows us to be reflective about the process without losing confidence in our ability to see things through to the end.

Describe your most successful attempt at ridding yourself of past anger. What helped you to be successful then?

How can you apply what you learned then to your current experience?

How will your life be different when you finally let go of your anger? Be specific.

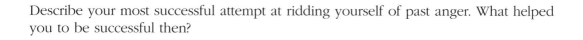

Spiritual Reflection

> The experience of disillusionment is different. Here it was not one's fellow man . . . but fate itself which seemed so cruel. A man who for years thought he had reached the absolute limit of all possible suffering now found that suffering has no limits, and that he could suffer still more, and still more intensely.[4] VIKTOR FRANKL

Each week during the fall semester of the 1997–98 academic year, I took a short trip to the country to join in a faith-centered study group. I looked forward to these weekly gatherings as a time to trade the usual frantic pace of life for the warm company of friends who shared my thirst for spiritual growth. Toward the end of one of our sessions, a gentleman in the group, attempting to illustrate a point, asked me if I had a brother. This was the first time anyone had asked me such a question since Michael had died. My mind raced trying to come up with an honest and accurate response that would not sound melodramatic.

"I used to," was all I could reply.

"Would he need a name tag for you to recognize him?" he inquired.

As this question hung in the air, without warning, a slide show started in my mind's eye. I stood at my brother's bedroom door staring at the lone figure resting on the bed. The figure was mostly bald with sporadically spaced, short black hairs accentuating its skull. Propped up on a pillow that lay by its right side was an outstretched arm that appeared to be twice its normal size. Through a morphine haze, the figure was talking softly to itself, occasionally punctuating the conversation with weak gestures of its left hand. A wave of shock and despair flowed through me as I braced myself for one of our last visits; I did not want Michael to see the depth of my pain. As I called his name softly the figure smiled the crooked smile that was Michael's signature. It was here that the slide show stopped as I struggled to gain control of my thoughts and rejoin the group.

Embarrassed and dismayed at this unwelcome interruption, I smiled weakly and gave the man the answer I knew he expected. "No, my brother wouldn't need a name tag." During the five minutes that it took for the meeting to come to a close, I summoned every ounce of my strength to pretend all was well. I said my good-byes, relieved at last to slip out of the meeting and into the front seat of my car. Alone there in the cold darkness, I whispered aloud the question, over and over, "Would my brother need a name tag for me to recognize him?" Deep from within came the gut-wrenching answer. "Yes. Yes, he would." The cancer and its subsequent treatment had so ravaged Michael's body that he was not immediately recognizable to me. Within seconds of this realization hot tears welled up in my eyes and spilled over my cheeks, blurring my vision as I slowly drove home. Ironically, the tears did not stop for two days as I relived the final forty-eight hours I spent with my brother.

Desperate to find relief from the pain, I journaled every detail I could remember about the experience. I reasoned that if I no longer had to depend on memory alone to recall those final cherished hours, I would be able to rest. Trust in my instincts paid off; the intense sorrow that had plagued me receded incrementally with each line I wrote. In its wake, however, was the clear realization that catastrophic loss had destroyed a very important part of my life. I hated the fact that the devastation could, of its own volition, create a slide show that started in my mind, without warning. I hated the fact that I could not command my emotions to do as I wished, but instead had to play victim to their need for release. I hated the fact that I had to watch my brother die, but most of all, I hated the fact that I would never be the same again.

Without my choosing, life had careened out of control and ended up in a desolate, sun-parched canyon filled with the dry bones of broken dreams and lost hope. Fueled by the pain of loss, my anger became palpable. As its enormity became evident I realized that I did not have the strength or the desire to daily carry its toxic burden. So I prayed fervently for the ability to release my anger and entreated God to replace it with the simple trust that emerges from knowing His desire to reach out to us in any and all circumstances. As the days and months passed, the anger slowly subsided, and then finally disappeared as I learned to quietly sit at God's feet, trusting in Him regardless of the whirlwind created by life's ever-changing circumstances.

People often express the idea that anger and spirituality cannot coexist. What are your thoughts about this? How does your belief impact your ability to deal with your anger?

In your sketchbook, draw a picture that represents your struggle with the relationship between anger and spirituality.

In relation to your loss, what anger issues do you continue to struggle with spiritually?

Meditation

A gavel echoes the grim night's verdict
Tireless pleas of a soul forever changed
Beg to return to yesterday for but a moment
To gather its meager belongings

Look beyond yesterday, O soul
To discover His storehouse overflowing
Even though transformation has had its way

The sun will rise again
To give birth to a new morning
With promises of deeper joy
And more splendid sunsets
DIANE DEMPSEY MARR

Summary

Catastrophic loss and its ensuing anger have the potential to either bring clarity and direction to life or destroy our peace if left unattended. Given anger's power and its potential impact on grief recovery, it seems wise to expend the time and energy necessary for thorough resolution. During this process we have the opportunity to explore anger's many dimensions, create suitable outlets for its expression, and finally release its hold. Spiritually, we discover a vital source of assistance as we share our burden with a loving and compassionate God.

As you worked through this chapter, what did you learn about the anger resulting from your loss?

On a scale of one to ten (with one being least and ten being most), rate the degree of difficulty you are experiencing with anger.

_____
1   10

Does your rating warrant seeking assistance from a licensed professional counselor or psychologist? After making your decision, consult with two people who know you well and would be willing to give you honest feedback about your need for help.

You may want to consult chapter 8 if you desire professional support for dealing with your anger, as it contains important information about the process of seeking this aid.

RECOMMENDED READING

Chapters 5, 6, and 7 of *A Grace Disguised,* by Gerald Sittser

Chapter 5 of *The Courage to Grieve,* by Judy Tatelbaum

Part 3 of *Where Is God When It Hurts?* by Philip Yancey

C•H•A•P•T•E•R   F•O•U•R

Our New Best Friend

Bargaining with Loss and Its Pain

And in the shadow of Thy wings I will take refuge,
Until destruction passes by.
(PSALM 57:1)

Rugged Territory

The journey thrust upon those who experience catastrophic loss is one that few embark on willingly, and for good reason. The geography of recovery's landscape, at least on the principal leg of the journey, is strenuous. Disbelief, shock, and anger cause the path to quickly ascend to the highest of elevations, where air is thin and mountaintops are jagged. Its rugged terrain demands that travelers outfit themselves to negotiate virgin territory that promises untold challenges under energy-sapping conditions. Trail markers warn of potential pitfalls ahead but do not elaborate about the intricacies of survival. People must discover their own unique solutions as they attempt to negotiate obstacles along the way. All of this must be survived before experiencing occasional interludes of rest most prominent in the middle and final stages of the grief recovery process.

The trials inherent in traversing through recovery's initial territory often appear as formidable opponents to healthy grief resolution. Progress is slow and, at times, our feelings of hopelessness seem more than we can bear. Despite challenges, most of us continue to trudge ahead. As we stand at the precipice of acceptance, some of us choose to make one final attempt at reconstructing our situation, in hopes of returning to the world we cherished prior to loss's spree of destruction. Denial, disbelief, and anger finally give way to bargaining.

Just like a life raft, bargaining boasts of its capability to shelter us from the frigid waters of loss and return us to the safety of the shore. Becoming its passenger brings with it the promise of reversing misfortune by restoring our previous sense of balance and peace. Bargaining represents our last-ditch effort to control the repercussions of our circumstances, to turn the tables on fate, to somehow have a voice in the final outcome of our predicament. Bargaining is another way of articulating our firmly held belief that loss can only happen when we give it permission to happen. But can we, or should we, really trust bargaining's vow to protect us?

Taking a Closer Look

To answer this question, we must first explore several facets of bargaining. *Bargaining* can be defined as the process of forging a mutual agreement between involved parties, with specific terms and clearly defined responsibilities. It may be pursued either for personal advantage or as a means to assist significant others. With regard to its role in the grief recovery process, bargaining is a normal human response that supports the belief that escape routes are plentiful. Despite the fact that loss appears imminent or has already occurred, there is always something that we can do to mitigate grief's powerful punch. Consider these examples:

A drug-addicted mother promises to stay clean in exchange for healing her baby who was born with a drug-related disability.

An executive promises to lead a moral life if her investors could be spared impending financial ruin that might result from her inappropriate and irresponsible use of their money.

A man promises to die peacefully if he is given enough time to hold his first grandchild in his arms.

A husband promises to end his two-year involvement with Internet sex if his wife and children are spared the trauma of discovering his unfaithfulness.

An older brother plans to devote his life to humane service if God will spare his little brother from the sexual abuse the older brother was forced to endure when he was younger.

Regardless of its basic premise, the creativity of its terms, or its targeted benefactor, bargaining seeks to escape loss's sting by nullifying its consequences or avoiding the psychological pain that accompanies it.

Review the bargains you have entertained during your lifetime. Now fashion your own personal definition of *bargaining*.

Describe bargains you have made related to your current loss.

Exposing the Essence of Bargaining

> Suddenly we are face to face with the fact that our "control" of life was only an illusion. Such a possibility is too frightening for most of us to accept easily; we feel as though our very survival is at stake, and we typically fight hard to keep our illusions intact.[1] DONNA DAVENPORT

We humans would like to believe that we possess the ability to manage all aspects of life, which is one reason why the act of striking up a bargain in the face of loss is so common. At the very core of bargaining is the hope that escape is possible, that by some fortunate twist of circumstances we will be granted power over our situation, and thus have the opportunity to shape the outcome to fit our needs. Essentially what we are attempting to do is to mitigate loss by nullifying the consequences of any number of actions or events, including:

Accidents   Irresponsible behavior
Bad decisions   Lapses in judgment
Criminal acts   Natural disaster
Displays of strong negative emotions   Oversight
Failure to intervene   Poor planning
Illness   Self-centered conduct

Examples abound of our attempts to cancel out loss's repercussions. The following story illustrates this point.

A young single mother, strapped for money, allowed her new boyfriend to baby-sit her two young children so that she could hold down a job. The arrangement seemed to be working well until one day when the nine-month-old was taken to a local emergency room to be treated for a broken leg. The boyfriend convinced medical staff, as well as the young mother, that the broken bone was the result of an accident that happened during play. Satisfied with the explanation, the mother continued to allow her boyfriend to baby-sit.

Several months passed before a second incident involving the infant occurred, once again requiring medical intervention. This time, however, the baby had sustained a closed head injury so severe that the damage was irreversible. His mother wept bitter tears as she was told that her son would never walk or talk, play with friends, or meet the girl of his dreams. Instead he would be relegated to a life of suffering, unaware of his surroundings and racked by frequent seizures.

To say that this mother was deeply grieved is an understatement. Now homebound to provide round-the-clock care for the baby, guilt plagued her daily as she witnessed his struggle to stay alive *(illness)*. She wondered how she could have trusted anybody with her children *(bad decision)* and how she could have missed the telltale signs of impending disaster *(failure to intervene)*. Pain, anguish, and remorse wore down her spirit, and finally, her desire to live. She reasoned that she did not deserve to live because of her failure to protect the baby *(lapse in judgment)*, so she pleaded with God to restore the youngster's health in exchange for her own. Even though the boyfriend had been able to fool trained medical staff, she still believed that she could have done something to prevent the tragedy.

This sad story highlights the human desire for control. Having such a valuable tool at our disposal, control promises to protect us, and our loved ones, from harm.

Bargaining is our way of attempting to impose order in a sometimes chaotic and unpredictable world. It can be fashioned as a means to escape the consequences of our own behavior, or that of others. It is also a vehicle by which we can manufacture a pact with fate designed to fend off the randomness of natural disaster, accidents, and crippling health problems. Ultimately, bargaining hopes to spare us from:

Anxiety	Embarrassment	Humiliation
Apprehension	Exposure	Pain
Blame	Fear	Remorse
Condemnation	Guilt	Shame

In reviewing some of the bargains you have made in the past, what types of consequences and feelings did you hope to avoid?

What personal beliefs allowed you to make those bargains?

Identify influences in your life that supported the beliefs you listed.

In your sketchbook, draw a picture of the disappointment and fear that you experienced when your bargains failed to bring about the results you had hoped for.

Giving Up Illusions

Bargaining is another way of articulating our firmly held belief that loss can only happen when we give it permission to happen. Coupled with this is the difficulty of giving up the idea that we can somehow effect change, especially when we have benevolent reasons for wanting to do so. Consider the following example.

> The father of a rebellious adolescent worries about the doors of opportunity that have been slammed shut by the child's irresponsible conduct. The dreams of college, a comfortable lifestyle for the child, and future grandchildren seem less likely with each passing day. All attempts to reason with the teenager having failed, the father makes one last attempt to salvage his vision. Convinced that his preoccupation with work is to blame for the child's behavior, the father turns to God with the promise of substantially increasing family time in exchange for the bright future he wants for his child.

What behaviors have you promised to increase or decrease in exchange for bargaining's promise to help significant people in your life?

It is also difficult to give up the illusion of control when having it would enable us to protect ourselves, or our loved ones, from the randomness of malevolent or criminal acts.

> Living in the middle of a busy metropolitan area, a middle-aged jogging enthusiast attributed five years of problem-free runs to the safety precautions she has faithfully observed, such as:
>
> ▶ avoiding poorly lit areas,
> ▶ wearing modest clothing, and
> ▶ refraining from the sexual banter so common among her coworkers.

In the jogger's eyes, her best friend was the bargain she made to practice safe behavior in exchange for protection. But can bargaining really be her new best friend; does it possess the necessary qualities?

True, enduring friendship is a treasure; it makes no demands and combines unconditional caring with a willingness to be vulnerable. Bargaining, however, can hardly be considered in these terms. It preys upon our deepest fears, promising to protect us from ruin. Rather than embrace us unconditionally, it offers its friendship in exchange for our life. It demands much, pledges much, and delivers little. In the end, we are disappointed to discover that bargaining's promises were powerless.

What positive habits have you promised to engage in to secure protection for you or your loved ones?

Look again at the jogger's bargain. What if, despite consistently practicing safe behaviors, she was assaulted during one of her nightly runs? What would she tell herself about her bargain then? Bargaining fails to prove itself to be the good friend it had originally portrayed itself to be when loss actually becomes a reality. The horror of randomness strips away our confidence in the belief that, if we live an upright life and do all the right things, we will be spared from pain and grief. Even though we may be willing to go to great lengths to fulfill our part of the bargain, such effort does not eliminate the possibility that catastrophic loss may occur.

What feelings emerge as you reflect on your limited ability to ward off loss?

What personally held beliefs are challenged when you reflect on your limited ability to control circumstances?

Brainstorm a list of new beliefs that have the potential to more effectively reflect the reality of your limits.

Stepping Out

> When we are no longer able to change a situation . . . we are challenged to change ourselves.[2] VIKTOR FRANKL

Beliefs supporting the idea that we have ultimate control only serve to frustrate us. With the illusion of successful bargaining squelched, we begin to wonder how we ended up taking such a wrong turn. A portion of our difficulty is born out of limited vision, and the narrow focus we bring to problem situations constricts our ability to survey the entire tapestry of our life. Rather than reflect on the current challenge as eventually becoming an integral part of a rich fabric, we instead dwell on the downside of uninvited change. As "bargainers" we are unable to fast-forward to the future to preview the rich products that result from trials; and because we lack vision, we are unable to imagine the true splendor that will be revealed when our tapestry is complete.

Reflect upon your past trials. In terms of character building, identify some of the gifts that resulted from your experience.

Were these gifts something you knew you would receive at the time of your loss? Describe how this knowledge could help you to accept your current trial.

If the desire to control limits the overall picture we are able to see in terms of our circumstances, what then will it do when we ask the question, "Who is in charge?" Our overwhelming need to feel in control, particularly in the face of loss, convinces us that we are in charge of our world and the happenings within it. Laboring under this false premise, we panic at the thought of the many details we must attend to. If our world is to run smoothly, we must gather adequate resources, gain the cooperation of others, and be sensitive to timing. Given that we are mere mortals confined by limited power and resources, it is no wonder we become frightened by loss and its implications. What could we possibly do to control an uncontrollable situation? Even if we did manage to successfully direct traffic today, what about the road ahead? What about tomorrow? The simplicity of the solution to this dilemma is astounding: Ask God!

When you feel as though it is your responsibility to take charge over your loss, what kinds of details concern you?

How does this situation change when you are willing to let God take charge?

Today, what can you do to invite God to be responsible for your life?

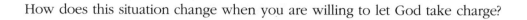

Spiritual Reflection

> When common sense says that life is frozen in a black block of despair,
> when the pundits say there is no answer, when even theologians tell you that
> God has abandoned us to our fate . . . may grace be to you, as the amazing
> promise that your future is open to God's surprising will for your good.[3]
> LEWIS SMEDES

Spring mornings hold the assurance of warmer days as winter's chill gradually subsides.
The appearance of April's newly budding flowers typically awakens in me the antici-
pation of the full bloom of summer, with its leisurely days and crisp, star-filled nights.
On the morning following my brother's passing, however, I found myself distracted and
unable to grasp the usual enjoyment I felt at this time of year. Checking in at the airline
ticket counter, I made my final preparation for the trip back home. As the plane carried

me toward my destination, I noted that other passengers went about their lives as though nothing of significance had recently changed the world. For the first time, feelings of isolation and loneliness overwhelmed me.

Upon arriving home, I was struck by the contrast of being in an environment far removed from the one in which my loss had unfolded. All seemed to be peaceful and in its place, again as though nothing about the world had changed. It was comforting and reassuring to be with my husband, as he understood the depth of my loss. I quickly became immersed in work and family life, hoping to hold back the flood of painful emotions that threatened to breach my wall of protection. This bubble of safety was short-lived, however, burst by yet another phone call informing me of the latest devastation to further unravel the once happy lives of my parents. As the conversation progressed I found it hard to believe that God would allow my family to be challenged by yet another loss.

Bothered by pain in his shoulder and side, my father sought medical advice. When initial treatments failed, concern for his well-being heightened and more tests were ordered. As the details of the latest dilemma swirled in my head, I worried that I did not possess the resources needed to deal effectively with the new onslaught of problems. Distance and the responsibilities of home and work magnified my concerns, at the same time preventing me from offering the direct support I knew my parents needed.

At this low point I turned to God, soliciting His cooperation with the bargain I was about to propose. Sizing up the situation that had transpired over the past several months, I reasoned that my family should be spared from further loss because we had courageously dealt with the recent deaths of two of our members. To ask that we sustain yet another blow to our flagging ranks would be excessive and unfair. My bargain with God encompassed the idea that I would do my best to handle the losses that had occurred up to this point, sharing what I learned with others, if only He would spare me and my family from further devastation.

To me, this seemed a reasonable request, in that I did not ask to escape the tragedy already experienced, but for the time to heal and rebuild resources that had been severely depleted. Further medical testing, however, slowly gave way to the awful realization that what my family was facing would, in short order, end yet another life. The darkest scenario possible had been uncovered and the only option we had left was to secure hospice services in hopes of making my father's final journey as comfortable as possible. Ten days after the medical community had given him six months to live, my father slipped away.

My bargain proved impotent in the face of certain death. No amount of wheeling and dealing could turn back the inevitable course of destruction. I would have to accept my powerlessness in the face of change, trusting God to equip me to successfully negotiate the rough road ahead. Taking the next step meant that I would willingly suffer the deep pain of loss. As I stood at acceptance's door, I was reminded of God's promise to accompany me on my journey through the valley of the shadow of death (see Psalm 23:4). I would not be alone, but instead could depend on the company, guidance, and steadfast love of my Maker.

Describe any bargaining you have engaged in with God during the course of dealing with your loss. What impact has this had on your spiritual life?

As you reflect on the bargains you made, identify the feelings you experienced upon realizing that God may not be cooperating. In your sketchbook, draw a picture or create a collage symbolic of these feelings.

It is not unusual to be angry with God when He does not do what we request. Talk to two other people who have experienced loss and compare notes. What ideas and feelings on this theme do you have in common with others?

Describe any difficulties you now have in trusting God to take care of you and your loved ones in the midst of adversity.

Record the names of at least three people you could talk to about these difficulties.

Meditation

> We must never forget that we may also find meaning in life even when confronted with a hopeless situation, when facing a fate that cannot be changed. For what then matters is to bear witness to the uniquely human potential at its best, which is to transform a personal tragedy into a triumph, to turn one's predicament into a human achievement.[4] VIKTOR FRANKL

Feelings of despair need not hoard the precious emotional energy we must spend on grieving. As we draw closer to acceptance, hopelessness takes flight as our perception shifts. What once created discouragement now yields itself to the possibility of new discovery. It is not human longing for wholeness that is to be faulted, but our definition of *wholeness* that must surrender itself to the process of transformation. Wholeness cannot be maintained by a strain of external circumstances resistant to change. Rather, wholeness is internally cultivated by a trusting heart that believes all things—abundance as well as excruciating loss—can be used to produce a more meaningful existence.

> The cloak of laughter long since gone,
> Exposed are all of the things gone wrong,
> And deep inside your soul you long to be whole,
> Deep inside of your soul.[5] DIANE DEMPSEY MARR

Summary

Bargaining with grief and its pain is a common occurrence in our struggle to overcome loss. At the core of this practice is the mistaken belief that we have the ability to control the circumstances surrounding our loss by making promises that reflect either some type of change within ourselves, or by offering charitable services and goods. In an attempt to protect ourselves or our loved ones, we contract with an external entity—another person or God Himself—to offer up something of value in exchange for a reprieve from loss's devastation. In the end, however, when bargaining fails to bring about the desired outcome, we are forced to face the reality of catastrophic loss. It is at this point that we become willing to accept our loss and depend on God's resources, rather than our own, to sustain us.

As you worked your way through this chapter, what was the most surprising thing that you discovered about yourself?

As you stand at the brink of acceptance, what are the greatest challenges that lie ahead?

Review your progress toward the development of resiliency traits. Which traits can you use to support your progress during the next phase of recovery? How will you apply these traits to the challenges that lie ahead?

RECOMMENDED READING

Chapters 8 and 9 of *A Grace Disguised,* by Gerald Sittser

A Grief Observed, by C. S. Lewis

Embracing the Darkness

Accepting Loss and Managing the Pain That Follows

Cast your burden upon the LORD,
and He will sustain you.
(PSALM 55:22)

Nightfall Approaches

Creativity and tenacity are both hallmarks of the human spirit. When applied to the challenges of life, these qualities have the power to transform even the most bitter of circumstances into palatable fare. Catastrophic loss, however, proves resistant, at least in the early stages of grief. Having set its course, it blindly rumbles ahead, refusing to heed the voice of reason. Denial has failed to banish loss, as did arguing with God. Anger did not shrink the growing reality of loss's destruction, nor did bargaining soften its impact. Without a substantial fortress in which to hide, defending against the acceptance of loss appears futile. The only logical alternative left is to reach beyond our fears to embrace our destiny. Tumultuous feelings of ambivalence confuse us. One minute we are sure that adopting an attitude of acceptance will secure our survival. The next minute we are convinced that it will ultimately lead to our destruction. Our ambivalence only increases as we attempt to listen to the many voices of advice. Despite wrestling with confusion and raw fear, we somehow find the courage to move forward. As we take our first tentative steps, depression instantly appears to greet us at acceptance's threshold.

Depression is a normal response during the middle stages of grief recovery. Even with our willingness to accept catastrophic loss, we can become somewhat frustrated to realize that acceptance is a *process* and not the *event* we had hoped for. With the world as we knew it forever transformed, we are called to reformulate our recipe for a happy existence. The challenges of gluing the broken pieces of life back together wear us down both physically and emotionally. It is no wonder then that depression becomes a familiar companion, for with our feelings of helplessness also come feelings of hopelessness.

The Faces of Depression

The type of depression that accompanies our initial brush with acceptance does not boldly announce its entrance into our lives, but slowly seeps into our existence over time. Neither is it the sort that is as easily managed as the occasional "blue funk" we all have experienced. The depression that now confronts us illuminates the sadness we feel in letting go of a cherished dream, person, or possession. As depression settles in for the night, we can't help but worry if we'll ever again see morning's light.

According to mental health experts, the following signs reflect the possible presence of depression:

- ▶ Persistent sadness
- ▶ Loss of energy (or fatigue)
- ▶ Inability to enjoy activities that, in the past, have been pleasurable
- ▶ Decreased interest in physical intimacy
- ▶ Excessive weight increase or decrease
- ▶ Inappropriate or excessive guilt
- ▶ Feelings of worthlessness
- ▶ Thoughts of harming oneself or ending one's life

Record the symptoms of depression that you are experiencing. Give examples for each.

Turn to a blank page in your sketchbook. Now close your eyes, and with your non-dominant hand, draw a picture that represents your depression.

Most, but not all, episodes of depression are transient in nature, disappearing once we discover a new balance for our life. But how concerned should we be about the episode that never seems to fade? It is important to remember that symptoms of depression are experienced along a continuum. Our degree of concern should take into consideration the following three-part formula.

> The kind and number of symptoms experienced
> + The degree to which each symptom is experienced
> + The length of time over which symptoms have consistently occurred
> = Degree of concern

Less serious symptoms, such as weight gain or feelings of guilt, experienced in their milder forms for brief periods of time do not warrant serious concern. In other words, not all depression requires the attention of trained professionals. Milder forms can often be managed with the application of a few simple tools (these tools will be shared later in this chapter).

However, if you become concerned because your symptoms persist and seem more difficult to manage, it is best to consult with a mental health professional who can help you to determine whether your depression requires a planned intervention. Licensed professional counselors and licensed psychologists both possess the skills necessary for such a task. As stated previously, chapter 8 offers some helpful guidelines for finding competent mental health assistance.

> Without hesitation you should immediately seek help for:
> ▶ suicidal thoughts,
> ▶ thoughts about harming yourself or someone else, or
> ▶ a persistent inability to function adequately at home, in social circles, or at work.

In addition to consulting a mental health professional, you should consult with your physician for several reasons. First, he or she can rule out any physiological condition that might better explain your symptoms. Second, if you have had an ongoing professional relationship with your medical provider, he or she is in an excellent position to help you determine whether or not your symptoms represent a dramatic departure from how you typically function. And third, should it be determined that your level of depression requires intervention, your doctor can explain the various options. A combination of both counseling and medication has been proven effective with moderate to more severe forms of depression.

Are any of your depressive symptoms concerning you? If so, why?

Record the name and phone number of one physician and one mental health professional who you are willing to contact, should it become necessary.

Use clippings from several magazines to create a collage in your sketchbook that represents your concerns about the depression you are feeling.

> Recovery is a misleading and empty expectation. We recover from broken limbs, not amputations. Catastrophic loss by definition precludes recovery. It will transform us or destroy us, but it will never leave us the same.[1]
> GERALD SITTSER

In addition to an awareness of depression's symptoms, we need to understand other factors of our loss that play into how severely depression may affect us. As the old saying goes, forewarned is forearmed! Three main components influence the degree of impact, and thus the level of depression we are likely to experience as a result of catastrophic loss.

1 **The Magnitude of Our Loss**
With an increase in magnitude, an increase in depression is likely.

2 **The Responsibility We Feel in Terms of Its Cause**
With an increase in responsibility, an increase in depression is likely.

3 **The Degree of Potential for Restoration**
With an increase in potential for restoration, a concurrent decrease in depression is likely.

Consider the following example.

A teenage girl who was sexually assaulted by a neighbor not only experiences the physical pain and humiliation of the event, but also loses her sense of safety, youthful innocence, and ability to trust. (The magnitude of her loss reaches astronomical proportions.) Because she blames herself for the attack, she is plagued by feelings of shame, guilt, and low self-esteem. She should have done something, anything, to stop the attack. (Her sense of responsibility is great.) A sense of hopelessness prevails as she tells herself that she can never again be like normal girls. (The potential for restoration, at least in her eyes, is minuscule.)

Weighing the girl's perception of all three factors, we would predict that she is struggling with a high degree of depression. However, we must also consider mediating factors as we attempt to determine the level of impact. These include:

▶ the number and quality of resources she has at her disposal,
▶ her degree of resiliency, and
▶ other challenges she was managing at the time of the loss.

Now let's play out the preceding example with two different sets of mediating factors to see how the level of impact can affect the degree of depression.

Girl A comes from a household with ample financial resources and an optimistic atmosphere. Her parents, who are very supportive, take immediate measures to protect their daughter, obtain therapeutic services to address the abuse, and shelter her from any additional challenges for a reasonable length of time.

Girl B, on the other hand, comes from a home whose limited resources are committed to the care of a disabled sibling. Although her parents are supportive, they rarely exude optimism and are often distracted and tired by the challenge of managing the special needs of the other child. Girl B chooses to keep the assault a secret, not wishing to further burden her parents.

When compared to Girl B, Girl A is less likely to experience severe depression because she enjoys full support from loved ones and has been given opportunities to work through her loss. The isolation experienced by Girl B is less likely to result in a happy ending. She will have to depend on personal resiliency alone to overcome her loss. Chances are great that she will experience severe depression for some time to come.

This example highlights the fact that mediating factors have the potential to either protect us from loss's full impact or put us at greater risk.

Reflecting on your loss, address each of the components that influence your degree of depression.

Magnitude:

Responsibility:

Potential for restoration:

Identify the mediating factors surrounding your loss.

Resources:

Resiliency characteristics:

Other challenges:

How have these mediating factors impacted your level of depression?

Which of the mediating factors can be used to further alleviate your depression? Develop a plan to put your ideas to work.

Managing Depression

> Since the hole is so enormous and your anguish so deep, you will always be tempted to flee from it. There are two extremes to avoid: being completely absorbed in your pain and being distracted by so many things that you stay away from the wound you want to heal.[2] HENRI NOUWEN

Realizing depression to be a normal part of the grieving process, it is essential to become equipped with valuable knowledge and tools to manage its impact on our lives. Just like a houseguest who never intends to leave, depression slowly becomes irritating and even annoying as it saps our energy and steals our hope. Rather than passively accepting this condition as something we just have to live with, we can instead find ways to actively combat depression's sometimes suffocating influence.

In his review of major counseling theories, educator and author Gerald Corey highlights two easy-to-use tools that have proven useful in managing depression.[3] In this section, you will learn how to put these tools to work for you. Although the techniques cannot remove the deep sense of sadness we feel as a result of our loss, they can help us cope more effectively.

TOOL NUMBER ONE: IDENTIFYING THINKING ERRORS

A crucial aspect in managing depression is related to the way we think. What we tell ourselves about any given event has a significant impact on how we act and feel. If, for example, we convince ourselves that we are to blame for all of our spouse's bad moods, we are likely to feel worthless and unlovable. If these feelings persist, we become susceptible to depression. According to Corey, the therapist and author Aaron Beck, along with several of his colleagues in the field of cognitive therapy, identified a number of errors in people's thinking that they believed to be the root cause of much of our emotional upset. Dr. Beck believes these errors in reasoning color not only the way we think about any given situation, but also how we respond emotionally. That's why knowing the main categories of these "mistakes" can help us to evaluate our thinking and identify ineffective beliefs that may be foundational to our depression. Consider each category and the examples provided.[4]

1. Black or White Thinking. This type of thinking resists evidence that gray areas are possible. Extreme positions are taken, with middle ground ignored.

> I must be a competent parent, perfect in all aspects of child care. There is no room for mistakes.

This parent does not take into consideration the typical learning curve for parents nor does he consider the resiliency of children.

2. I Am My Past. This type of thinking narrowly focuses on our past mistakes and character defects, causing us to define who we are today in negative terms.

> Because I caused the car accident, I am not a competent defensive driver and should never drive again. I'm too irresponsible.

This person bases her opinion about her driving ability on an isolated accident that happened years ago.

3. It's All About Me. This type of thinking convinces us that events that take place outside of ourselves are really all about us.

> God sent the tornado to punish me for being a selfish person.

This person personalizes an event of nature.

4. The Terrible, Horrible, Huge Big Deal. This type of thinking greatly magnifies the importance of an action or event.

If I had not promised her new swim fins and goggles, she would not have thought about swimming in the lake. I am responsible for her accident.

This person gives too much power to an innocent comment.

5. *Once and Forever.* This type of thinking convinces us to generalize beliefs about one event to other unrelated events.

Because I blew my cool, I lost my position at that electronics plant a few years back. I am not too surprised that others see me as incompetent and impulsive.

This person believes that one "failure" has the power to cancel out the growth he has made since that time.

6. *The Negative Filter.* This type of thinking invites us to draw our conclusions from isolated details so that we lose sight of the general context of the issue.

I can't believe I said all of those things to my own mother. She will never be able to think of me as a good person again.

This adult child dwells on a negative comment she made to her mother about a sibling, and ignores the extensive and compassionate assistance she gave to her family.

7. *Out of Thin Air.* This type of thinking rummages around in the basement of our imagination, drawing conclusions without solid facts or evidence.

It will be the end of the world when my husband finds out that I am unable to conceive. I'm sure he will leave me, because all he ever wanted in life were children of his own.

This wife fails to consider that her husband values other aspects of their marital relationship and might be open to considering other alternatives to create a family.

Which of these thinking errors seem most familiar to you?

Reflecting on your loss, identify specific thoughts, beliefs, or conclusions that fall into one or more of the seven categories of thinking errors. Explore their impact on your level of depression.

TOOL NUMBER TWO: As Easy As ABC

Another tool that can assist us in managing depression complements Beck's identification of thinking errors. According to Corey, renowned theorist Albert Ellis believes that we create much of our own unhappiness by the way we think. Dr. Ellis advances the idea that the anger, frustration, sadness, and depression we experience are due, in large part, not to the precipitating event, but to what we tell ourselves about it. His "ABC" theory highlights two main sources of negative thinking (and how to replace them with more functional thinking). The first source springs from absolute imperatives such as "I should" or "I must," which directly lead to negative self-judgments. The second source of negative thinking reflects the belief that the world "must" be a certain way if we are to lead quality lives. This type of thinking feeds disappointment when things do not turn out the way we think they should.[5] Consider the following examples.

It is all my fault! I should have let him buy the new truck. If I had, he would have been sitting up higher and would have seen that other car. He would not have gotten into that accident.

If this disease robs us of our retirement dreams, life won't be worth the effort.

In each example, chances are great that the speakers will experience such feelings as guilt, anger, self-condemnation, disappointment, or hopelessness. Dr. Ellis believes we can equip ourselves to combat these negative feelings by learning to dispute what he calls irrational beliefs. The next set of statements portrays another way of looking at the situations.

Having another vehicle would not have prevented the other driver from crossing the double yellow line and hitting his car.

We may have to alter our plans because of this illness. We may not be able to do exactly what we wanted, but there are still plenty of enjoyable alternatives.

It is obvious that the latter two statements are less likely to create negative feelings, and thus depression. So how do we get from the negativity of the first two thoughts to the realistic optimism of the second two? Logic is the key! We have to sort through our thinking and test its validity. Dr. Ellis offers the following simple formula.

Disputing Formula	**Application**
A = Activating event	*aspect of our loss*
B = Belief about the event	*belief about "A"*
C = Consequence (emotional or behavioral)	*anger, fear, anxiety, sadness*
D = Dispute the belief	*dispute "B"*
E = Effect	*new effective philosophy*
F = Feeling (new)	*hopeful, relieved*

We have an opportunity to alleviate some of our depression when we challenge beliefs about different aspects of our loss. By applying the formula, we learn to take a critical look at these beliefs by asking ourselves if they are logical, valid, or even useful. Consider an example of how this formula can be applied to catastrophic loss.[6]

A couple in their late thirties had been trying to conceive for three years. Just when they were ready to consult with fertility experts, they found themselves pregnant. Excited and relieved, they prepared for the birth of their first child. The pregnancy progressed smoothly until the delivery. Last-minute complications prevented the baby from receiving adequate oxygen and resulted in permanent brain damage. Overcome with sadness and concern, they brought the infant home and tried to put together a plan to care for the child's special needs. As the days turned into weeks, the young father struggled with overwhelming grief, self-condemnation, and feelings of inadequacy. Because he avoided taking care of the baby for fear of causing greater harm, his marriage also suffered. Depressed and exhausted, he made an appointment to see his counselor.

As the counselor and young father worked through details and feelings surrounding the loss, they discovered several beliefs that were preventing the father from embracing parenthood.

One belief, in particular, seemed to be the most problematic. Together they applied the disputing formula.

A = Activating event: Dream of having a normal child

B = Belief about the event: Because I am sad about fathering a disabled child, I am a bad person who does not deserve any children.

C = Consequence (emotional or behavioral): I am experiencing guilt and depression and am avoiding childcare.

D = Dispute the belief: Most people hope to have a normal child. Many parents of disabled children learn to adjust, deal with their sadness as it surfaces, and are still great mothers and fathers.

E = Effect: I can be a good father regardless of the child's challenges.

F = Feeling (new): I am very sad that my child struggles; this is hard to watch. I have a lot to learn about fathering this child, but I am a quick learner.

As the father began to understand the impact of his ineffective belief on his thoughts, feelings, and behavior, he made it a point to remind himself that many other parents of disabled children shared his sad feelings. Doing so helped to both reduce his depression and give him the confidence he needed to reach out to his child.

With your primary loss as the focus, use the ABC formula to identify and replace a belief that is not helping to reduce your depression.

A = Activating event

B = Belief about the event

C = Consequence (emotional or behavioral)

D = Dispute the belief

E = Effect

F = Feeling (new)

Thinking now of the cascade of loss that followed your primary loss, identify another belief that may be causing your depression to worsen, and then apply the ABC formula.

A = Activating event

B = Belief about the event

C = Consequence (emotional or behavioral)

D = Dispute the belief

E = Effect

F = Feeling (new)

By applying Dr. Ellis's step-by-step formula, we are able to analyze our negative thinking and correct illogical or invalid thoughts. In replacing the type of thinking and beliefs that are harmful to our sense of well-being, we have an opportunity to see life from a more accurate vantage point. At first this new point of view may feel somewhat awkward. That's to be expected! In exchanging depression-producing thoughts and beliefs for more functional ones, it will take time and practice before our new way of thinking feels natural. Just remember this good news: Your feelings will eventually follow your new beliefs! It's just a matter of time.

Spiritual Reflection

Faith means believing in advance what will only make sense in reverse.[7]
PHILIP YANCEY

Grief carries with it the incredible power to transform once mundane tasks into memory capsules potent with strong emotion. Whether intense joy or profound sadness, memories recalled during the early stages of acceptance challenge us to begin the process of integrating loss into our daily life. This ongoing endeavor highlights both the treasured aspects of the past and the stark absence of a person, a job, or a dream of today. The fact that loss's erosive power has the ability to change lives can no longer be denied.

Several months after the deaths of my brother and father I took a trip to the local stationery store to pick out greeting cards for family and friends who would be celebrating October birthdays. I had taken this trip numerous times in the past and always enjoyed finding the perfect card for each person. As I surveyed the choices, my eyes suddenly fixed on the family section where the word *brother* appeared on a number of cards. Michael had been born on October 28, 1950, four years and three days before me. As small children with birthdays so close together, we were afforded the pleasure of prolonged celebration and multiple birthday cakes. As I silently stood before the display, tears began rolling down my cheeks. Never again would there be a need to buy a birthday card for my brother. I would forevermore remember him on a different occasion: April 7, 1997; the day he died.

A few weeks after the episode in the stationery store, I received a birthday card from my mother. Sadness overwhelmed me as I stared at her lone signature at the bottom of the card. With my father's "Love, Dad" blatantly absent, I realized that never again would I receive a card that contained his warm wishes or his beautifully scripted handwriting. The once neutral experiences of exploring a stationery store or receiving a birthday card were transformed into emotional events reminding me that life had spun out of control and would never again be the same. With each sad revelation my depression deepened. The cushioning effect of denial now gone, I stood alone to face the ever-growing darkness. During this stage in my recovery, tears came easily. I could not take care of grief's business in one simple transaction. Instead, I was forced to grieve each discovery of change separately.

At times such as these I was so very grateful for the many resiliency factors that helped me to cope: the support of good friends and family, understanding colleagues, and my inherent tenacity. I was especially thankful for my faith. Having become a Christian in my mid-twenties, I was acutely aware of what life could be like without the comfort, direction, and assistance of a loving God. My faith made it possible to accept the present circumstances with their subsequent pain because I knew that somehow my depression would lift, and God would reveal a means by which healing and hope could once again permeate my existence. This knowledge did not neutralize the pain of loss, but it did help in managing the fear I sometimes felt when depression threatened to overtake me.

Beyond the emotional landslides of triggered memories, beyond fear and depression, God graciously offers us a means by which loss can be woven into the fabric of our life. What is it, then, that we must do to become the beneficiary of such a splendid offer? There is no magic formula to discover, no test to survive, no special group to join before we can enjoy the fruits of God's promises. He simply asks us to change our focus—from the worrisome circumstances of this life to the steadfast love of a Father who desires to give us His best. It is not the flawless progression of life that buys us our sense of tranquility. It is the expansion and transformation of our soul that causes us to more readily accept the peace that has been available to us all along.

Describe how ordinary things (a song, an anniversary date, or the like) trigger sadness and exacerbate your sense of loss.

At this stage in the grieving process, when acceptance's depression becomes a familiar part of daily living, what spiritual challenges concern you the most?

List the resiliency factors that originate from your spiritual life and describe how you might use them to support your recovery.

◤ Meditation

> For I am confident of this very thing, that He who began a good work in you will perfect it until the day of Christ Jesus. (Philippians 1:6)

The dark night's apparition whispers to our imagination, convincing us that whatever lies beyond loss is not worth having. But its repeated attempts to drown out the voice of hope only serve to expose its ghostly countenance. We cannot be bound by the chains of darkness when we focus on the intrinsic beauty of night itself. It is rare that natural eyes would recognize the simple elegance of God's perfect plan, for they are not equipped to do so. But the sparkling stars of a moonlit night, seen through spiritual eyes, reveal a glimmering hope that speaks to the very core of our souls; He has a plan for our lives. In the sweet solace of God's presence we learn that, not only is there life after loss, there is *abundant* life.

Summary

Acceptance and depression seem to go hand in hand as we face the grief born of cat-astrophic loss. Embracing depression as a normal part of recovery, however, does not mean that we must stand helpless before our deep sense of sadness. By increasing our general understanding of depression's role in the grief process, we are better able to cope with our own unique experience. We cannot escape depression's pain, but we can equip ourselves with realistic expectations, self-help tools, and spiritual support that will ease the burden of sadness. As we look forward to the days ahead, we are assured that our depression will gradually give way to brighter tomorrows.

In completing this chapter of your workbook, what helpful information did you learn?

With regard to this stage of the grief recovery process, which aspects concern you most and why?

Make a list of questions that will help you address your concerns. Discuss these with a friend who could help you identify potential resources to aid your recovery.

RECOMMENDED READING

Chapter 11 of *How Can It Be All Right When Everything Is All Wrong?* by Lewis B. Smedes

Chapters 6 and 7 of *The Courage to Grieve*, by Judy Tatelbaum

Part 4 of *Where Is God When It Hurts?* by Philip Yancey

One Last Mountain

Life-Changing Challenges Encountered in Recovery

Blessed be the LORD, because He has heard the voice of my supplication.
The LORD is my strength and my shield; My heart trusts in Him, and I am helped.
(PSALM 28:6-7)

A New Dawn

In the initial period following catastrophic loss we spend a great deal of time agonizing over our ability to survive the resulting carnage. Challenging days become so routine that the only way to tell them apart is by the degree of distress we experience. But now, having outlasted the worst of the storm, we venture outside of our shelter to greet the possibility of brighter days. Transition through the stage of acceptance has begun. The oppressive depression we encountered earlier in the grief process begins to subside as we become anchored in the fertile soil of new understanding. While we can continue to expect bad days, good days appear with increasing frequency. Rather than expending the majority of our energy maintaining survival status, we now are able to free up a portion of our resources for growth-oriented exploration.

Recovery's major assignment now centers on reorganization. Important tasks before us include redefining who we are and clarifying a new guiding philosophy for our lives. What once we thought important we may now judge as trivial. Relationships with family, friends, and God take precedence over our former need for control and the accumulation of possessions. We marvel at the petty circumstances of days gone by that distracted us from the sacredness of our existence. We are better able to take things in stride and less willing to let the daily grind of life rob us of our joy. In addition, we are more discriminating about how we expend energy, pushing aside past ruminations about earthly unfairness that ultimately diminished our vitality. It is as though we are given a new lens of discernment through which we are better able to identify the very essence of life itself.

This heightened awareness illuminates a new set of challenges that had previously been obscured by the initial chaos so typical of catastrophic loss. No longer hampered by the intense pain of early grief, obstacles that threaten to block our complete recovery come to the forefront. Just when we thought we had finished the bulk of our grief work, we are once again called back to the task of identifying and reconciling issues. Problems such as increased feelings of isolation, old hurts, and difficulty in releasing ourselves and others in forgiveness all beg for attention. A mountain of challenges looms in the distance, but this time we possess a hope that previously eluded us. Because of our recent experience, we know we are equipped to conquer the highest peak—to not only survive these difficulties, but to grow as a result of them.

Alone with Aloneness

> People who are suffering, whether from physical or psychological pain, often feel an oppressive sense of aloneness. They feel abandoned by God and also by others, because they must bear the pain alone and no one else quite understands.[1] PHILIP YANCEY

Catastrophic loss and feelings of isolation seem to go hand in hand. The degree to which these feelings are exacerbated depends on a number of different factors and the type of loss. Other influences that come into play include a society that fails to acknowledge the long-term effects of loss and the mistaken notion that we can rid ourselves of the basic human condition of aloneness. Impatience with people who are grieving seems to seep from the very pores of our cultural norms. As previously discussed, after a modest length of time, we are expected to turn our attention to the necessities of life and living. Society's admonishment to do so is delivered in many forms:

▶ Keep a stiff upper lip!
▶ Pull yourself up by your bootstraps!
▶ Just do it!
▶ It's time to get over it!

Sources of pressure vary; friends, family, coworkers, and even strangers urge us to move on but fail to offer us a means for doing so. Without a lifeline we are overtaken by the swelling waves of grief.

Describe some incidences in which you felt pushed by others to get on with your life.

What kinds of feelings resulted from this type of pressure?

The urgency with which we are pushed along is likely to be powered, at least in part, by feelings of discomfort and sadness harbored by others. Our pain recalls in them the unresolved pain of their own past losses. At other times, it may simply be that others do not want to be inconvenienced by our less-than-stellar performance as we go about the task of juggling responsibilities and mourning our loss. Regardless of the reasons, the reactions of those around us may sometimes create intense feelings of aloneness, rushing us into silence where fear, abandonment, and powerlessness stay trapped just below the surface. Understanding the anxiety or impatience of others may serve to soften the intensity of our feelings and add perspective.

As you reflect on situations in which people silenced your pain, what types of challenges might they themselves have been experiencing?

How does understanding other people's issues impact your feelings of aloneness and isolation?

As unpleasant as they are, feelings of isolation and aloneness are very typical in the early and middle stages of grief recovery. Even when encountering those who have lived through similar circumstances and are willing to allow us to express our pain, we soon discover that shared understanding has its limits. Because no two people experience loss in the same way, we ultimately own a unique and separate piece of misfortune's misery. This reality highlights the truth that each one of us, even in community, is essentially alone.

Describe the contrast between sharing your loss with those who *have* and those who *have not* experienced a similar circumstance.

As you seek support from those who understand your dilemma, what pieces of your loss do you continue to feel are yours alone?

In your sketchbook, draw a picture or create a collage that symbolically represents the feelings that emerged when answering the preceding question.

As you reflect on the reality of the human condition of aloneness, what feelings and concerns come to mind?

Name at least one person you can talk to about this issue.

Like the fledgling unsure of its wings or its ability to navigate the vastness of open skies without assistance, we perch on the edge of aloneness wondering if we will survive. Reluctantly taking flight, we quickly realize that we have the capacity to continue on with life even in the shadow of aloneness. Although it will always be with us, we can soar nonetheless, discovering meaning even in our solitary state.

What meaning, if any, does the reality of aloneness bring to your life?

Unfinished Business

> The pains we dare not remember are the most dangerous pains of all. We fear to face some horrible thing that once hurt us, and we stuff it into the black holes of our unconsciousness where we suppose it cannot hurt us.[2]
> LEWIS SMEDES

Surprisingly, the most challenging part of finishing our business with loss is knowing when it is final. When will we know our journey is at long last completed? Though we have dealt with many issues along recovery's road, it is likely that several more remain. Much like peeling the layers of an onion, our awareness of issues emerges only as previous layers of difficulties are stripped away. Lurking in the distant recesses of our mind, these dilemmas patiently wait their turns; and as they linger, they transform themselves into formidable barriers to grief's resolution. Just what do these issues look like, and how do they prevent our growth? Unresolved issues come in many forms; consider an example that illustrates different challenges that can grow out of these issues.

> Even though a man believes he has worked through major issues connected to the neglect he experienced as a child, his feelings of mistrust persist. This man made an honest effort to explore different facets of his childhood neglect, including parental disinterest in meeting basic emotional needs. He has yet, however, to come face to face with the mistrust which grew from his experiences, and thus has little insight into its poisonous effect on significant relationships. Mistrust has driven a wedge between him and those he loves, evidenced by the fact that he constantly questions his wife's motives and restricts his children's activities to those he can closely monitor. Feelings of fear and anger plague his family as they struggle to please him and calm his fears. Deep down, feelings of worthlessness and fear of rejection plague him, so he uses bravado to cover up his insecurities.

Before this man can believe in himself or be free of mistrust's power, he must be willing to go back to his childhood to embrace the little boy who hungered for love but did not receive it. Only then will he come to realize that the neglect said much more about his parents than it ever did about him. Ultimately, he must mourn the loss of a little boy's dream to have parents both loving and worthy of his trust. As his grief is resolved, mistrust will slowly melt away as he becomes more able to separate his past from the present. Completing the grief process gives him an opportunity to view life from a healthier vantage point, and to begin healing significant relationships.

What issues have you successfully dealt with up to this point in your grieving process?

Are there other issues you are aware of that must be resolved?

Name two people you can trust who would be willing to help you explore the possible existence of additional issues.

What feelings well up inside of you as you become willing to look at the unfinished business connected to your loss?

There is little doubt that unfinished business has the power to restrict our existence, stifle our joy, or leave us with scant hope for a better tomorrow. How then can we track down such an underhanded culprit who hides itself in the bushes along recovery's road? We may not be able to pinpoint the exact location of our captor, but we can stay alert to hints of its presence reflected in our patterns of behaving and thinking. Following are several examples of behaviors and thinking patterns that work to block grief resolution.

- ▶ We persistently try to change a situation over which we have no control.
- ▶ We ruminate over old hurts, waiting for other people to make amends.
- ▶ We remain entangled in old issues, allowing them to impact today.
- ▶ We play out old issues over and over again, in hopes of writing a new ending to our story.
- ▶ We tell ourselves that we can't move on until "X" happens.
- ▶ We stay focused on the unfairness of our loss, and feel resentful of people who appear to have easier lives.

In reviewing these behavior patterns, do you recognize any that may reflect your current thinking or behavior?

Can you identify any other behaviors that may indicate you have unfinished business to address?

Develop a plan to address your unfinished business. What type of help should you seek to develop and implement your plan? How and when will you get started?

By identifying patterns of thinking and behaving that may indicate the presence of unresolved issues, we have an opportunity to explore new aspects of loss that previously escaped our attention. Working through these issues, we become better able to translate the meaning we have attached to our experience. New insights then empower us to heal the pain of the past and move closer to fully integrating our loss. Even though understanding is the first step toward freedom, it may not prove powerful enough to propel us beyond one of the most common obstructions to personal growth—unforgiveness. Many of us find that letting go of old issues is not as easy as it sounds. When it comes to forgiveness, we get stuck.

What challenges have you encountered when attempting to forgive?

The Process of Forgiveness

Forgiveness is love's toughest work, and love's biggest risk. If you twist it into something it was never meant to be, it can make you a doormat or an insufferable manipulator.[3] LEWIS SMEDES

Forgiveness would be so much easier were it not for unforgiveness, its clever and divisive twin. Unforgiveness can be likened to a parasite; it feeds on the anger and hurt of its host, finding its most satisfying nourishment in human pain. It thrives on the cycle of replayed scenes, recalled anguish, and rehashed justification for holding fast to grudges. Essentially, unforgiveness grows plump on our desire for revenge. The pall it casts over our lives causes us to underestimate beauty's power to lift us above the mire and to overestimate retaliation's ability to give us back our lives. While we are distracted with entertaining numerous ways to get even, unforgiveness pilfers our joy and unobtrusively steals our soul bit by bit. Before it is too late, before we are drained of our desire for goodness, we must find a way to extricate the parasite. Forgiveness provides us with the only means to move beyond the past and regain both our perspective and vitality. We must learn to forgive those we believe to be the cause of our pain, including God. Perhaps most difficult of all, we must learn to forgive ourselves.

Describe the thoughts and feelings that emerged as you read about unforgiveness and its power to block our growth.

Open your sketchbook to a blank page. Now close your eyes, and with your nondominant hand, draw a picture of the destruction and unhappiness created by unforgiveness.

Whether at the center of our loss or on its periphery, acts of omission, as well as acts of commission, have the potential to create pain. When connected to catastrophic loss, this pain seems to multiply as our world crumbles around us. Being the injured party, we find it difficult to believe that others did not anticipate the impact of their actions, or lack of action, on our now fragmented lives. Incredulous, we blink back our disbelief with the hope that we can somehow turn back the clock to recapture life as it once was. As the reality of loss's permanent status sinks in, we are catapulted into a struggle that will require our forgiveness before we are allowed to go free.

But if forgiveness is such an essential ingredient in grief's resolution, why do so many of us balk at the task? Why don't we forgive as soon as we realize there is something to forgive? I believe we wrestle with forgiveness because of our natural inclination to protect ourselves. If we are to be honest, forgiving represents a huge risk. We worry that guilty parties may see our forgiveness as a green light for further abuse. We fear that we will once again be run over by cruelty and callous disregard. If forgiveness prevents those responsible for our pain from learning a much-needed lesson, why then would we dismiss them from school? But when, at last, reason and grace overtake, we come to understand that forgiveness is the only choice that can bring miraculous healing to both the wronged and the wrongdoer.

In the first column, make a list of people connected to your loss whom you need to release in forgiveness. In the second column, give a short explanation of why you need to forgive them. Finally, in the third column, describe why you have yet to forgive them.

People I Need to Forgive	Why I Need to Forgive	Why I Have Yet to Forgive

Make a list of the difficulties created by your unforgiveness.

Now describe the benefits of forgiving each person you listed.

For all persons listed, describe the type of healing that you hope forgiveness will bring to your life as well as theirs.

How can you prepare yourself for the actual act of forgiveness, and how will you convey your forgiveness to the people you wish to forgive?

Forgiving ourselves is often a more challenging task than forgiving others. This is especially true when we hold ourselves to a standard of perfection that few humans could achieve. We endlessly wrestle with our insecurities, repeatedly question our own motives, and agonize over our inability to be better people. Exhausted from the battle, we collapse under the weight of our shame. Before we can heal, we must be willing to set aside the "super hero" expectations and embrace our inherent frailties and shortcomings. Coming to this place—finding self-acceptance—is not an easy task, but it *is* possible. With the help of others who care, we can, little by little, let go of our inappropriate expectations. As we approach the threshold of acceptance, the door of forgiveness quickly swings open to offer us the inner peace that has eluded us.

In the first column, list the things connected to your loss for which you need to forgive yourself. In the second column, describe the unhealthy standards that have blocked this possibility. Finally, in the third column, describe healthier expectations that can open the door to forgiveness.

Things for Which I Need to Forgive Myself	Standards That Keep Me Stuck	More Reasonable Expectations

Describe the difficulties that have resulted because you have been unable to forgive yourself.

Now describe the benefits that you will enjoy as a result of self-forgiveness.

Sometimes we find ourselves stuck and unable to go forward even though we *have* forgiven. This may indicate that additional issues beyond our awareness remain. The following example illustrates this concept.

> After ridding herself of anger and forgiving her husband, self-doubt continues to plague a woman who was abandoned for a younger, more attractive partner. She agonizes over what she could have done differently: how she should have dressed, taken better care of herself, or been more interesting. As she continues to work through her issues, the truth begins to surface: she married a man who closely resembled the father whose high expectations were impossible for her to meet. Her father's conditional love had left her feeling inadequate and filled with shame. Now face to face with the core problem, she realizes that there is still more work to do. She must release her father in forgiveness before she can be completely free herself. Forgiveness has become a complex issue as the layers of hurt have accumulated over time.

Are you aware of other hurts that may somehow be connected to your present loss?

Given the additional challenges shared above, is there a specific need to forgive your-self or others?

Considering the complexity of layered issues, what type of therapeutic support would you like to receive?

———

Spiritual Reflection

Finally, brethren, whatever is true, whatever is honorable, whatever is right, whatever is pure, whatever is lovely, whatever is of good repute, if there is any excellence and if anything worthy of praise, dwell on these things. (PHILIPPIANS 4:8)

Because catastrophic loss often occurs without warning, many of us are robbed of the opportunity to achieve the closure we so desperately desire when our relationships come to an end. Unlike those whose loved ones are unexpectedly snatched away by death, I feel fortunate to having been able to say a proper good-bye to both my brother and father. Although the active role I chose to take during each man's illness left me with many vivid and painful memories, I experienced a sense of peace following their deaths. There was no sadness about unfinished business, or remorse over things I should have or could have done. Because I gave them both what I would have wanted had I been the one with terminal cancer—a willing partner for life's final journey—I could mourn my loss without the heavy burden of regret. However, there remained for me one unresolved issue connected to the circumstances that ultimately led to my father's death; the challenge set before me would require me to forgive a faceless and unrepentant foe.

In my father's initial attempts to address his illness, medical staff compiled a thorough history, hoping to uncover clues that would make sense of his symptoms. Specifically, they were searching for possible irritants that could have been responsible for the difficulties he was experiencing. An autopsy later confirmed what physicians had suspected for several months: the rare form of respiratory cancer from which my father suffered was caused by exposure to a type of insulating material he had encountered during his years of work. Upon learning of these results, I began to search the literature in hopes of understanding the situation that surrounded the manufacture and use of this product. What I soon discovered would kindle a fire of rage within me that would take months to extinguish.

According to the sources I reviewed, manufacturers knew at least twenty years prior to my father's exposure that the insulation material had the potential to cause serious illness. Despite this knowledge, the product continued to be sold to companies whose unsuspecting employees would be required to handle the material—a decision that affected thousands of lives.

The idea that an unknown group of people had recklessly gambled with my father's health—choosing monetary gain over the sanctity of human life—enraged me. How could anybody with even a minuscule amount of decency be so cold, calloused, or greedy? This and other questions plagued me.

What was most troublesome to me was the fact that those who had made the fate-filled decision were faceless. There was no one person to confront, no office door to bang on, only the insulting silence of a handful of manufacturing companies whose reluctant apologies came in the form of monetary settlements forced on them by the courts. It was not an act of good faith that curtailed the use of this product, but rather the result of legislation designed to protect a naive public. How could I begin to forgive such evil? Why would I even want to?

As the days turned into months, my anger grew until finally even I was no longer enjoying my own company. Regardless of what wrongs had been done, I had to somehow resolve the issue so I could move on with my life. It all came down to one simple choice. I could either: (a) continue to hold the guilty hostage and feed my growing anger and unhappiness, or (b) release the faceless executives in forgiveness. The first choice, I reasoned, was pointless. How could I, one lone voice, right the wrong done to a multitude of victims? Avenging my father's death was impossible, as I could not imagine any type of earthly punishment sufficient in magnitude to even the score. The second choice seemed even more far-fetched. If I somehow managed to forgive my invisible foes, would I then be required to let them off the hook? In my mind, they did not deserve such leniency; but deserve it or not, this is what I chose—not for their benefit, but for my own. This option appeared to provide the best chance for ridding me of anger's burden.

I knew that I did not have the power to dispense forgiveness on my own. The task loomed as a dark, towering mountain before me. I would need an able partner for this venture. In the quiet of meditation and prayer I approached God, admitting my inability to let go, and asking for the strength to forgive from my heart. This did not mean that I ignored the wrong done, nor did it mean I pretended all was well. It did mean, however, that I willingly left the fate of these companies in God's hands, trusting Him to administer justice as He saw fit. In doing so, I broke the dam that had constrained me, releasing positive emotional energy that directed my attention back to all that was right with life. In God I found the freedom and strength to forgive the faceless foes that had hastened my father's death.

As you grow through acceptance, what remaining challenges would you like to turn over to God?

Challenge #1:

Challenge #2:

Challenge #3:

Look ahead five years into the future. What will your future look like if you choose to handle these challenges on your own?

In your sketchbook, draw a picture of the feelings that emerged as you answered the preceding question.

What do you hope to accomplish for yourself by turning over your challenges to God?

Make a plan to turn over each of the challenges you listed.

Plan for Challenge #1:

Plan for Challenge #2:

Plan for Challenge #3:

Name two people you can trust to give ample spiritual support while you carry out your plans.

Meditation

> At that moment there was very little I knew of myself or of the world—I had but one sentence in mind—always the same: "I called to the Lord from my narrow prison and He answered me in the freedom of space."[4] VIKTOR FRANKL

Loss soberly announces its imposed ban on any possibility of returning to our previous state of existence. Our best hope, we fear, is to somehow manage life with whatever meager resources we have left. However, what initially appears to be a simple attempt to survive loss's destruction slowly reveals itself to be a creative process that urges us forward toward the realization of a deeper and more meaningful existence. As we struggle to reinvent our lives, we are filled with both dread and awe—dread of the unknown that lies ahead, and awe as we begin to recognize the beauty of our new surroundings. This is no typical academic course in which we are enrolled. It is an apprenticeship of the heart designed to shape in us the extraordinary characteristics of God, the Master Craftsman. We are not left to accomplish this task alone, but instead we can trust Him to be our wise and compassionate mentor.

Summary

New issues that emerge in the middle stages of grief recovery challenge us to look deeper at loss's influence on our life. At this perilous crossroad we can call upon God for help and strength. As we grow to accept our aloneness, address each difficulty, and release others and ourselves in forgiveness, we begin to feel substantial relief from our once massive burden of pain. The winds of change carry us, lighter now, to a new land where we have the opportunity to reconstruct our life in a richer and more meaningful way.

After working through this chapter, describe your hopes of feeling "lighter."

As you think about reconstructing your life, what things are you looking forward to?

RECOMMENDED READING

Chapters 10, 11, and 12 of *A Grace Disguised,* by Gerald Sittser

Parts 1 and 2 of *Forgive and Forget,* by Lewis Smedes

Chapter 11 of *The Courage to Grieve,* by Judy Tatelbaum

Part 5 of *Where Is God When It Hurts?* by Philip Yancey

A Strand of Gold

Integration of Loss and Joy's Renewal

But as for me, I shall sing of Thy strength;
Yes, I shall joyfully sing of Thy lovingkindness in the morning,
For Thou has been my stronghold, and a refuge in the day of my distress.
(PSALM 59:16)

Wisdom's Light

With the majority of grief's work completed, we finally arrive at a place where we are able to reap the rewards of our labor. The difficulties and challenges of the mourning process recede into the background as our awareness of personal transformation emerges. A deep sense of satisfaction and acceptance replaces the anger and depression so prominent in the earlier stages of grieving. With increased energy and fewer distractions we are now able to take up the task of *integration*. What exactly does it mean to integrate loss into our life and how will we know when we have successfully accomplished this task?

Integration does not insist that we forget our experience nor does it translate itself to mean the absence of pain or sadness. Genuine integration does reflect, however, that we have successfully worked through our grief to such a degree as to allow us to reengage in a full and satisfying life. The direction and length of the journey depends greatly on our individual circumstances and our ability to recognize and resolve issues. Full recovery also relies on our aptitude for cultivating and applying our own unique set of resiliency factors.

Much as the ocean's tide smoothes the rougher edges of nature over time, catastrophic loss transforms and refines our character. The way we now experience the world is significantly different from the way we experienced it before our loss. With wisdom as a comrade, we no longer flee from difficult questions. Instead, we embrace the fresh perspectives that unfold to enrich the quality of our life; we are more willing to wrestle with our fears, knowing that they do not possess the power to destroy us; and we feel better prepared to manage challenges should grief return, once again, to insist on being our companion. Although we do not invite further loss, we are better able to take in stride the ebb and flow of daily living.

This newfound wisdom has a way of putting things into perspective. It reminds us not only that we are capable of weathering storms, but that we may do so with the support of a caring community of others. It prompts us to look at all sides of an issue rather than falling back into the myopic view we may have possessed prior to our loss. As costly as it may be, wisdom earned through our trials has purchased for us the priceless gift of hope for a richer and more meaningful tomorrow. With each sunrise we become increasingly aware of the promise of new beginnings and the beauty that has taken hold in our heart.

The Metamorphosis

The soul enlightened understands, the soft heart sees the plan. Peace
that was so illusive now free to all who dare to look beyond the stars.[1]
DIANE DEMPSEY MARR

Our primal response to loss is to struggle *against* the changes it brings in an attempt to maintain the order we believe is central to our survival and happiness. We cannot imagine anything good being born out of something so painful and so we desperately search for a means to reverse reality. It is not long before we grow weary of the relentless skirmishes and are no longer able to keep change at bay. Tired and spent, we now find ourselves engaged in hand-to-hand combat with loss in a concentrated effort to stay the inevitable. With the passage of time we realize that our struggle *with* change, although at one time necessary, becomes redundant and counterproductive. We must receive loss and prepare to struggle *forward,* beyond the pain created by unwanted change. Acceptance being the only vehicle sturdy enough to transport us through integration's territory, we climb aboard trusting that we will be able to find our way. As we stand on the edge of our old world preparing to cross over to the new, a mix of hope and relief fills our mind. It has been a long, difficult road, but finally we can see our new home in the distance. Integration's promise of a better tomorrow is now within our reach.

In light of your experience with loss, describe what it means to you to struggle forward.

How do you envision making the final leg of your journey?

What resiliency factors do you possess that will assist you in the integration process?

For integration to occur, we must be willing to submit ourselves to change. Personal transformation is not a singular event; it is a gradual process that takes place over time. Much like the miraculous transformation of a caterpillar turned butterfly, we can expect to struggle through a series of recovery stages before we emerge as a fully integrated being. The caterpillar's task is one of change. This all-consuming work takes place outside the view of others, and inside the protective environment of its cocoon. Although change is not recognizable to those of us on the outside, we know that, given the right circumstances and enough time, a beautiful butterfly will eventually emerge.

Many of us become impatient with the cocoon stage. Unable to visualize its transforming power and integration's end goal, we fail to take the necessary time to heal and grow. We just want to get on with life; but try as we might, we cannot hurry the process. Tearing the cocoon apart to free the butterfly before it is ready results in the delicate insect's demise. It must remain within the confines of the cocoon, submitting itself to the process of change, until it is equipped to fly. In a similar vein, prematurely exiting the final stages of grief ultimately circumvents the necessary work that leads to successful integration. Perhaps we find the tasks of grieving too demanding or feel ill-equipped to manage the confusion and uncertainty. Even more worrisome, perhaps we fear that we will be destroyed by the pain inherently connected to the process. Regardless of our concerns, flight into wellness before the appointed time results in falling short of integration's mark. Consider some indicators of this state:

▶ Unresolved issues that inadvertently impact general adjustment; this may take the form of depression, anxiety, unnecessary guilt, vague fears, or phobias
▶ Unresolved issues that negatively impact our relationships with others
▶ Low self-esteem and a negative perception of our ability to solve problems

▶ Low tolerance for changes in our environment or relationships
▶ The development of resentments, bitterness, or unforgiveness
▶ A growing sense of pessimism, failure to find hope, or no vision for the future

Describe the occasions when you have been tempted to flee from complete resolution of your grief.

As you review your personal journey through recovery, are there any behaviors or thought patterns that may indicate incomplete resolution of your loss?

Just as early exit from the latter stages of grieving creates adjustment problems, prolonging the state of grieving also prevents us from achieving full integration of our loss. In short, we cannot arbitrarily lengthen the grief process without experiencing difficulties. Why would we choose to camp out in such an uncomfortable place? Why would we not want to move on? The following example may shed some light on this puzzle.

Mark is a middle-aged man who is experiencing difficulties in relationships with his spouse and children. Family members' complaints revolve around his inability to connect emotionally, and he does often use anger and silence to achieve distance from others, thus putting his marriage in jeopardy. After a childhood scarred by emotional and physical abuse, Mark is unable to let down his protective walls, even though he is aware of his aloofness and its source. Despite several years of counseling, Mark has not been willing to fully grieve the loss of his childhood because he does not want to do the energy-consuming work required. Instead, he chooses to stay stuck in the mire of his childhood, ruminating over past wounds.

If we are not willing to venture beyond the "caterpillar to cocoon" stage into the unknown skies of personal growth, we will find ourselves forever stuck in the grieving process. We must somehow find the energy and determination to fully immerse ourselves in change-related activity if we are to ever emerge from our loss as fully integrated human beings. The process is not an easy one, but it is a necessary ingredient in the recipe for emotional growth.

Are you aware of any issues that are keeping you from fully integrating your loss? If so, discuss several strategies that can help you move forward.

Sometimes, when we are able to envision the process of change unfolding, we have a better idea of how we can move forward. In your sketchbook, create a series of three pictures or collages that represent your process of change. Your first creation will represent the "caterpillar" stage.

Now create a representation of your experience during the "cocoon" stage of development.

Finally, create a representation of your emergence from the cocoon into the "butterfly" stage.

Describe the characteristics you can look forward to possessing after fully integrating your loss experience into your life (the emergence of the butterfly).

Back to School

> All I knew was this: Morrie, my old professor, wasn't in the self-help business. He was standing on the tracks, listening to death's locomotive whistle, and he was very clear about the important things in life.[2] MITCH ALBOM

With life as our classroom and grief as our teacher, we have the opportunity to grow in significant ways. As difficult as it may be to imagine ourselves as willing pupils of grief, we can learn important lessons from it. Just like any good teacher, grief encourages its students to learn from their experiences. Making meaningful connections between the lessons of loss and the way we live our lives is a major step toward building a firm foundation for a more satisfying existence.

Grief also supports student learning by imparting the skills of discernment. Having the ability to sort through life's many details to identify its most essential dimensions enables us to focus on what is ultimately important. The most complex of lives suddenly appears manageable when we allow ourselves the luxury of excluding the trivial from our range of vision. We become less concerned about raking leaves and more intrigued with the splendor of autumn. We are less bothered by what we do not receive from others and more determined to leave the lasting imprint of love on those to whom we are connected. Perhaps most important of all, we are less focused on living the easy life than we are on living a meaningful life.

Identify two people who know you well who can help you to identify major lessons learned throughout your recovery from loss. Describe those lessons.

In light of what you have learned in your recovery from loss, make a prioritized list of the most important things in your life. Include people, goals, and activities, and explain why you have arranged them in this order.

Before we are dismissed from school, grief reminds us that, despite rumors to the contrary, we can expect to discover the unexpected; the lessons we learned during our bout with catastrophic loss produced some lasting gifts. For many of us, this idea makes little sense. We have been so engrossed in issues of survival that we gave little or no thought to the possibility of positive outcomes.

Discuss any difficulties you have in viewing your loss as a source of "life gifts."

Despite our skepticism, grief invites us to entertain the possibilities. Closer inspection reveals not only the presence of multiple gifts but also a diversity of gifts as well, with no standard set of gifts distributed to those who would receive. Depending on personality and life circumstances, each individual's loss will produce unique treasures. For example, it is safe to say that the majority of us who have weathered loss learned the following lesson:

People and things we take for granted can slip from our grasp in the blink of an eye.

The type of gift that may flow from this lesson will depend on our individual characteristics. For those of us who struggle with procrastination, we may choose to change our behavior by no longer putting off telling those whom we love how important they are to us. If, prior to loss, we expected people to know how we felt without ever communicating the message directly, we may now determine a direct means to reveal our feelings. Or, if our happiness depended on material goods, we may be less willing to invest our energy in accumulating things and more willing to invest in people. Although we may learn common lessons, the gifts that flow from such are likely to look different.

Take an inventory of the "life gifts" that may have come to you through the lessons of loss. Explain the circumstances from which each gift came.

Now compare your inventory with someone who has experienced a similar loss. How do your gifts differ?

By intentionally recognizing the blessings that flow from the lessons of loss, we take another step toward fully integrating loss into our life. At first this may seem unnatural or difficult given the pain we have suffered. However, as we train our eyes to search for these gifts, the possibilities become increasingly apparent. Mingled with our pain from the past are the bittersweet seeds of future growth. As we plant these seeds we will no doubt witness a bountiful harvest.

Planting requires preparation. Make a plan for how you would like to use three of your gifts.

The Seasons of Grief

That is one of God's greatest—and most common—gifts: the gift of hope to keep us in the game, to return us to our places not as the same people we were before, but awake, alive to God's transforming presence in our midst.[3]
JAMES EDWARDS

Winter symbolizes the experience of catastrophic loss. We are forced to expend the majority of our resources to survive its harsh reality. As we cling to what little we have left, we remain steadfast in our desire to feel the warm rays of sunshine break through the gloomy, hovering clouds of loss. It is doubtful that any of us would survive our grief were it not for winter's promise. Gradually the signs of new life emerge, promising the hope and renewal that come with each new spring. We rediscover truths previously hidden by that season's darkness. We expend less energy in merely surviving the dark side of loss, while committing ourselves to the process of discovering its gifts. Best of all, we no longer feel like grief's captive as we begin to realize that we have the ability to choose our response to loss.

The idea that we possess the autonomy to shape our reaction to something outside of our control at first seems ludicrous. How can we manage something bigger than we are? Through an act of determination, willfully training our perspective, we can cultivate our ability to transform the dark lessons of grief into inspiration for personal growth.

I learned this truth while reading Viktor Frankl's book *Man's Search for Meaning*. I must admit that my initial reaction to Dr. Frankl's ideas was one of skepticism. But I wanted to remain open, and decided to engage in an experiment that would ultimately change my life. First, I made a detailed list of the losses I had experienced in my life, including those in childhood. After making my list, I then reviewed the circumstances of each loss to identify the gifts that had emerged from my pain. To say that the results of my experiment were powerful and transforming is an understatement. The exercise taught me that I, not loss, was in charge of the way I viewed and experienced the more challenging aspects of my existence. I had the freedom to choose how I would respond to loss as well as the responsibility to define its meaning. Embracing this truth took me out of the victim role and put me in the driver's seat. I did not have control over the terrain that loss chose, but I did have charge of how I would make the journey.

What kept you going in the darkest moments of your grief?

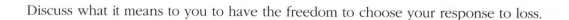

Discuss what it means to you to have the freedom to choose your response to loss.

In your sketchbook, draw a picture or create a collage that represents your freedom to choose your response to loss.

Considering what you have learned, how will this impact the way you will respond to future losses?

The freedom we have in choosing our response is the very same freedom that can support our desire for a fuller and more satisfying life. As we grow to accept the inevitability of change, we focus less on fear and more on the possibilities for growth. Future choices such as investing in other people, realizing a dream, or pursuing a satisfying vocation are no longer suffocated by "what ifs." Though aware that all things come to an end, we have the courage to go forward, knowing not only that we can manage loss when it occurs, but also that we can be forever enriched because of our experience. Accepting change frees up precious emotional energy that once was wasted on worry. More willing now to travel life's road in spite of occasional bad weather, we have the ability to cherish gifts given to us regardless of how long we can enjoy them.

How can you reduce your worry as you reach out to enjoy that which may be with you for only a brief time?

Looking to the future, describe the people (or things) in whom (in which) you wish to invest.

Make a plan to move toward those investments.

Spiritual Reflection

> Finally, we reach the point where we begin to search for a new life, one that depends less on circumstances and more on the depth of our souls.[4]
> GERALD SITTSER

Several months following the deaths of my brother and father, with the help of relatives and friends, my mother arranged for the placement of a memorial bench on the pier in Santa Cruz, California. Each year we have returned to the pier to enjoy the sights and smells of the ocean, to marvel at the adept fishing skills of hungry pelicans, and more so to remember the two men with whom we shared a significant part of our lives. I can still feel the powerful impact of seeing the bench for the first time. As I ran my fingers across the carved letters spelling out their names, childhood memories flooded my senses: fishing off the pier in hopes of catching dinner, studying the habits of various animals and birds, dining ocean-side in small, cozy restaurants; our family had spent many happy hours taking in the rich culture of the pier. A wave of sorrow engulfed me as I silently acknowledged that the recollections of yesterdays held no promise of shared tomorrows.

With each successive year my visits to the Santa Cruz pier have become less about what no longer is, and more about the gift of time spread out before me. As healing slowly mended the wounds caused by loss, God patiently instructed me in the art of recognizing and appreciating the sacredness of each new day. I have learned to celebrate and honor the past, allowing it to enrich my existence, while savoring the rich blessings of the present. I am more intentional about my relationships with family and friends, more willing to take advantage of opportunities to bless others, and more drawn to the pleasure found in simple things I used to take for granted. Rather than loss diminishing my desire to live life to its fullest, it has created in me a new willingness to engage life at an even deeper level.

After experiencing catastrophic loss, why would I want to take the risk of becoming even more vulnerable to grief's pain? What has breathed life into this emerging self? For me, the answer to these questions highlighted two significant words: *trust* and *God*. *Trust* has allowed me to dive deeper into life; that is, trust in *God* and in His unwavering love for humankind. God's hand of love has been abundantly apparent throughout my recovery process. On the occasions when I felt sure that grief would overcome me, that life was merely a succession of losses to survive, God entered in. He taught me to train my attention less on the difficulties of life and more on His eternal legacy of love. In doing so, I have found increasing courage for the journey, more meaning in ordinary life, and a stronger resolve to venture beyond my fear of loss.

God has proven Himself to be more than worthy of our trust. As we each look back on our unique journey through grief, we will recognize His hand of love in our healing process. God was the good friend who sat with us through the darkest hours. He was the hand of help that allowed us to glue the pieces of life back together. He was the steadfast and unwavering presence convincing us that despite the long, cold night, the promise of morning was certain. As we come to accept the cycle of life—the joy of new beginnings as well as the relinquishment of what was once cherished—He calls on us to savor and celebrate His love. We may not be able to trust life to be fair, or remain as we wish it to be, but we can trust God to be our ever-present and able guide through its many twists and turns.

As you look back on your journey through the recovery process, what events reveal God's hand of healing in your life?

Spiritually, how have you grown as a result of experiencing loss?

What spiritual questions remain as you attempt to make sense of the loss you experienced?

How do these questions impact your ability to trust God?

Identify two people with whom you can share your spiritual questions.

▶ Meditation

"And I will bring the third part through the fire,
Refine them as silver is refined,
And test them as gold is tested. They will call on My name,
And I will answer them; I will say, 'They are My people,'
And they will say, 'The Lord is my God.'" (Zechariah 13:9)

On the brink of hope's last breath the lone heart yearns for what cannot be. Off in the distance a spark ignites the parched dreams of yesterday, fueling the desire for a glimpse of tomorrow. The glowing embers of the Refiner's fire illuminate the beauty of heaven's handiwork—a tapestry of uncommon beauty woven with a rainbow of threads spun from life's seasonings and grief's earnest labor. And fused into the very soul of the ever-evolving fabric is a strand of gold.

Summary

Recovery from grief is the restoration of our capacity for living a full life and enjoying life without feelings of guilt, shame, sorrow, or regret.[5] JUDY TATELBAUM

Having come full circle, we regain our balance and a renewed desire to move beyond our loss. To fully engage in life once again, we must recognize the lessons and gifts embedded in our grief. Exercising freedom to choose our response to loss, we walk toward tomorrow with a deeper appreciation for today. The wisdom that comes with experience accompanies us on our continued journey, transforming the once barren desert into a rich land of promise. Although more loss lies ahead, we find reassurance in God's presence. It's this truth that allows us to continue to invest in life and living, always ready to embrace the possibilities for personal growth and the opportunities to bless others.

Describe your feelings about the preceding message.

Discuss further personal growth that will make it possible for you to fully engage in life after loss.

RECOMMENDED READING

Chapters 13, 14, and 15 of *A Grace Disguised,* by Gerald Sittser

Part 4 of *The Courage to Grieve,* by Judy Tatelbaum

Man's Search for Meaning, by Viktor Frankl

The Dream Tree, by Stephen Cosgrove

C·H·A·P·T·E·R   E·I·G·H·T

Eye of the Storm

Taking Care of Ourselves in the Midst of Loss

I will bless the LORD who has counseled me;
Indeed, my mind instructs me in the night.
I have set the LORD continually before me;
Because He is at my right hand, I will not be shaken.
(PSALM 16:7-8)

Recovery's Road Map

Few would argue with the fact that recovery's road is long and arduous, requiring great patience and energy. Because the process of working through grief cannot be hurried, we must be willing to let go of expectations associated with expedience. When we attempt to rush ahead of loss's pain, we unwittingly extend the length of our recovery process by creating additional difficulties that distract us from our main task. Although we may wish with every fiber of our being for the radiance of sunrise, we must accept the reality of the present darkness by preparing for the long night ahead. Wisdom would have us pace ourselves and carefully ration our resources.

Combating weariness and exhaustion means being aware of the demands that lie ahead and adjusting our expectations accordingly. Our sense of peace will not be restored quickly, nor will the balance we once enjoyed. As chaos reigns on the outside we are called to look inward to find tranquility's haven. In time we will come to understand our experience, but until we arrive at our destination we must find our satisfaction in traveling well. Taking good care of ourselves along the road—being intentional about self-care—means consistently attending to physical, emotional, and spiritual needs. Leaving all this to chance may prove to be grossly insufficient. Lack of sleep, poor eating habits, or limited time for reflection can deplete our cache of resources and act as a detriment to our progress. To ensure that there will be rest stops along the way, we need a road map.

Many of us balk when it comes to taking care of ourselves. We hurry to keep up with the usual pace of life, determined to go on regardless of the circumstances. Stopping to address a need could jeopardize our normal routine. But how can life be normal after catastrophic loss? To others, self-care sounds selfish, overindulgent, or even melodramatic. Carrying on with life in the usual manner seems most responsible—but is it?

If we stop long enough to survey the damage created by catastrophic loss, it becomes evident that we will need to make many repairs before life returns to some semblance of "normal." Especially true in the early and middle stages of recovery, simple coexistence with loss requires vast amounts of energy. Instead of expecting to keep up our old pace, we need to slow down long enough to fashion a plan that will protect and nurture our physical, emotional, and spiritual well-being. For many of us, this represents our first-ever attempt at intentionally taking care of ourselves. How then can we possibly know what we need? Observing others may serve only as a dim light, given that what constitutes good self-care for one person may be different for another. Determination and a willingness to experiment are the surest ways to develop a plan that fits our unique needs.

Constructing a Plan for Self-Care

> You have to keep moving, as you are doing. Live a faithful, disciplined life, a life that gives you a sense of inner strength, a life in which you can receive more and more of the love that comes to you.[1] HENRI NOUWEN

Most people who have experienced catastrophic loss somehow find a way to survive its destruction. The degree of difficulty that each person experiences depends on a number of different variables, as discussed in previous chapters. The most poignant question about grief's aftermath, however, has to do with quality of life. We survived loss, but did we survive it well? What is the difference between those who exist while barely hanging on by a thread, and those who seem to flourish despite the challenges, coming out intact on the other side of loss? Self-care holds the key to solving this mystery.

One of the best examples of human resiliency I have witnessed has come from walking alongside my mother these past few years. Despite losing her own mother to dementia, and losing both her firstborn child and her husband of fifty-one years to cancer, she has refused to give up. In these most difficult of times, I have watched her courageously embrace the grieving process, while at the same time forging a new life for herself. God has blessed her determination with a wonderfully rich blend of new adventures and relationships. My mother has not only survived, she has flourished! She has discovered ways to nurture her personal growth while consistently attending to more basic needs.

The best way to begin devising a plan for self-care is with what we already know to be true about ourselves and our needs. Ironically, loss has a way of derailing many good habits in which we normally engage. It is important to remember that the added stress of grieving requires us to go beyond our usual routines to balance out the increased emotional and physical demands encountered in recovery. The following questions will help you sketch out a broad foundation for your plan.

How many hours of sleep do you require to feel refreshed?

Given the stress of circumstances, what additional rest time do you need to stay healthy?

If you are having difficulty falling asleep or staying asleep, what can you do to improve the situation?

What does your diet look like when you are feeling your best?

What changes would you like to make in your eating habits that would help you feel better during this stressful time?

Describe your normal exercise routine.

Are there any adjustments you would like to make in your exercise routine to lighten depression or to help you sleep better at night?

If these adjustments represent a significant change in your exercise habits, it would be wise to consult with your physician before proceeding. When can you make an appointment?

Developing Healthy Boundaries

> A helpful way to understand setting limits is that our lives are a gift from God. Just as a store manager takes good care of a shop for the owner, we are to do the same with our souls.[2] HENRY CLOUD and JOHN TOWNSEND

Beyond the foundation of physical survival, there are other aspects of living that must be considered when building a solid self-care plan. Our desire for a sense of community and belonging must be weighed against the need for time alone to rest and reflect. Depending on the type of loss we have experienced, we can either find ourselves alone and feeling abandoned, or just the opposite, overwhelmed by the kindness of more people than we have energy to manage. Regardless of whether we deal with famine or feast, we are challenged to adjust personal boundaries so that our need for affiliation is met without taking over our life.

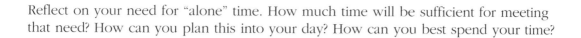

Reflect on your need for "alone" time. How much time will be sufficient for meeting that need? How can you plan this into your day? How can you best spend your time?

How do you currently meet your need for fellowship with others?

Would you like to adjust this in any way? If so, how?

Do any relationships in your life seem overwhelming? Explore ways to reshape your personal boundaries to make these relationships more manageable during the grieving process.

Consideration must also be given to achieving a healthy balance between time spent tending to responsibilities and time allotted to leisure and play. Although this might sound simple enough, the fact that we are worn out by grief's influence complicates matters considerably. Low energy convinces us that we are lucky to have met our responsibilities and survived the day; anything beyond this seems impossible. Unfortunately, when we make no attempt at play, we lose out on the therapeutic benefits of leisure activities. We ignore the very things able to nourish our soul: a walk in the woods, the sound of ocean waves, the beauty of a sunset, or the laughter of small children.

Do you have a tendency to put off leisure activities? If so, discuss why this is a problem for you.

As adults we are very familiar with the "responsible" side of our being. To get in touch with *all* of who we are, we must allow ourselves to play. In your sketchbook, draw a picture or create a collage that symbolizes your playful side.

What activities have you enjoyed in the past?

Are there any new activities you would like to experience?

Make a plan to fit at least one leisure activity into your week. Regardless of your energy level, make a commitment to follow through!

When we begin to attend to our needs, the strong connection between our physical, emotional, and spiritual self becomes evident. Each piece is an essential and integral part of our being; tending to one benefits the others. The care plan you just completed reflects this premise and highlights the important role we can play in enhancing our own well-being. In addition to self-care, there are times during the grief recovery process when reaching beyond ourselves is a necessary step in regaining our health. The following section not only speaks directly to this issue, but will also equip you to find the assistance that best meets your needs.

Reflect on your attempts at self-care and describe the connections you have discovered between your physical, emotional, and spiritual well-being.

Therapeutic Support

Sometimes "taking care of business" by ourselves is not enough. Perhaps we are experiencing some physical challenges or need a safe place to share our thoughts and feelings. Securing professional assistance can go a long way in smoothing recovery's path. Inevitably, we all encounter rough spots as we attempt to find our way through the difficult changes and emotions that accompany loss. With our physical and emotional selves taxed far beyond normal limits, it is wise to seek assistance from medical and mental health practitioners when we have questions or concerns about our physical symptoms or life circumstances. Identifying the right person to help us can sometimes be challenging, especially if we are unfamiliar with the services in our community. If there is anything I am passionate about in my own professional work, it is equipping people to be wise consumers of health care services. Whether looking for a medical doctor, naturopathic physician, or mental health practitioner, we need to consider a number of variables if we expect to achieve a good match between our needs and the services provided. Asking key questions beforehand can assist in making an informed decision.

Education

What school(s) did this practitioner attend?
Does the school have a good reputation?
What accreditation does the school, or program within the school, possess?
Related to the services provided, what degree(s) or certification(s) did this practitioner earn?

Training and Practice

Does this practitioner have any special training or experience with the issues for which you seek help?
Does this practitioner consistently engage in continuing education to keep abreast of changes in his or her field?

Quality Control

Is the profession guided by national and/or state standards?
Is there a governing body that receives consumer complaints or concerns?
Is the practitioner you are considering licensed to practice?
In terms of the professional community, is this practitioner a member in good standing?

Personal Philosophy and Business Practices

Is this practitioner able to describe the guiding philosophy foundational to the services he or she offers?
Is the expressed personal philosophy compatible with your values and needs? If not, is this practitioner willing to help you find another practitioner who can better meet your needs?
Is this practitioner's style of interacting comfortable for you?
For services to be helpful, what does this practitioner expect from you?

What do the fee schedule and billing guidelines look like?
Is this practitioner willing to work with your insurance company?

Consumer Feedback

What type of reputation does this practitioner have in the community?
Do current or past clients or patients recommend this practitioner?
Concerning this practitioner's professional behavior, have any complaints
    been lodged against him or her?

Answers to these questions can be found by contacting state agencies charged with the responsibility of overseeing various professions, or by using the Internet. General research focused on professional fields such as medicine, alternative medical care, psychology, or counseling will yield information about the basic philosophy of each field, education and training standards, ethical standards, and licensure or certification requirements. It is also possible to locate lists of educational institutions that adhere to the profession's accreditation standards. By logging onto the Internet, for example, and typing in "counseling.org," you arrive at the homepage for the American Counseling Association (ACA). ACA is a national organization whose primary membership is professional counselors. Information and links found on the ACA site focus on pertinent training and practice issues, as well as licensure standards. Other related professional organizations that work to develop and uphold professional education, training, and practice standards include the Council for Accreditation of Counseling and other Related Educational Programs (CACREP) and the National Board for Certified Counselors (NBCC).

Having obtained general information about the professional field, consumers are in a better position to choose a qualified practitioner. Information about individual practitioners can be gained from either talking to the practitioner's office manager or to the actual practitioner.

If, for example, you called my private practice office inquiring about my background, you would learn the following information about Dr. Marr:

► She graduated with a doctoral degree in 1991 from the University of Idaho, whose counseling programs are accredited by CACREP.
► She is a Nationally Certified Counselor (NCC) and an Approved Clinical Supervisor (ACS).
► She is a Licensed Professional Counselor.
► She is an active member of ACA, and from June 1997 to June 2002 has served as the chair for the Bylaws and Ethics Committee for the Washington Counseling Association, a state affiliate of ACA.

More in-depth information with regard to personal philosophy and business practices can be gained by making an introductory appointment with the practitioner. In addition to national standards, it is important to remember that counselors are bound by state guidelines that vary from state to state. In the state of Washington, mental health counselors must provide their clients with written information that explains the client's rights, billing and payment policies, and the counselor's treatment philosophy. In addition, clients are given a contact address and phone number in case they have any concerns about their experiences with the counselor. Professional counselors who want to conduct an ethical practice will gladly and openly discuss these issues with potential clients. It is my initial goal, for example, to determine whether a good fit exists between the needs of new clients and my ability to assist them in reaching their therapeutic goals. If I lack the expertise or embrace an incompatible philosophy, it is my responsibility to refer these individuals to someone who may better meet their needs.

Today, in addition to formal therapeutic services such as individual or group counseling, there are a number of economical opportunities to receive education and support. Counted among these services are support groups, which are typically organized around a particular loss issue such as:

- ▶ divorce,
- ▶ death of a loved one,
- ▶ families dealing with end-stage cancer,
- ▶ families of the mentally ill,
- ▶ fathers of severely disabled children,
- ▶ families with a loved one who is incarcerated, or
- ▶ parents of missing children.

Support groups facilitated by trained professionals usually have specific objectives that are met through a combination of education and informal discussion. Group exercises are often designed to equip participants with new coping methods to help ease the difficulties encountered during loss and recovery transition. In contrast, support groups facilitated by laypeople usually consist primarily of informal discussion, and are fashioned as a means to share useful information and give and receive encouragement. Both types of support groups are offered by a number of different sources, including:

- ▶ benevolent organizations,
- ▶ churches with social assistance programs,
- ▶ community interest groups,
- ▶ community mental health agencies,
- ▶ employee assistance programs offered as a job benefit,
- ▶ medical service groups such as hospitals and managed care, or
- ▶ private groups comprised of counselors, psychologists, and social workers.

If utilizing more than one source of support (regardless of whether it's counseling or informal assistance), it is important to create linkages between them. Without these linkages, services tend to be fragmented and less effective. In my work as a counselor in private practice, professional collaboration increases my ability to provide meaningful services sensitive to the physical, emotional, and spiritual health of my clients. For example, when a client gives me written permission to share information with his family doctor and dietician, I have an opportunity to become a partner in a holistic health care team that supports the unique needs of that person. I can monitor the effects of medication on mood or energy levels, reporting my observations to the physician; or I can help my client create a program that will help him adhere to the nutritional advice of his dietician.

What physical challenges have you dealt with since experiencing catastrophic loss?

Besides depression, what emotional challenges have you experienced as a result of your loss?

In your sketchbook, draw a picture that represents your struggle with these physical and emotional symptoms.

Which symptoms concern you most? Which symptoms concern the people closest to you?

At this point, what type of assistance do you feel would be most helpful?

If more than one type of service will be needed, how will you support collaboration between your health care providers?

When will you contact your health care provider to make an appointment?

If you do not already have a health care provider, use the format below to investigate your alternatives.

Recommendation of family, friend, or colleague?

Name: _____

Type of practitioner: _____

Contact number: _____

Comments about practitioner: _____

Now check the questions whose answers you consider to be essential in your decision-making process. Use a separate piece of paper to record the information you gather.

Education

___ What school(s) did this practitioner attend?

___ Does the school have a good reputation?

___ What accreditation does the school, or program within the school, possess?

___ Related to the services provided, what degree(s) or certification(s) did this practitioner earn?

Training and Practice

___ Does this practitioner have any special training or experience with the issues for which you seek help?

___ Does this practitioner consistently engage in continuing education to keep abreast of changes in his or her field?

Quality Control

___ Is the profession guided by national and/or state standards?

___ Is the practitioner you are considering licensed to practice?

___ Is there a governing body that receives consumer complaints or concerns?

___ In terms of the professional community, is this practitioner a member in good standing?

Personal Philosophy and Business Practices

___ Is this practitioner able to describe the guiding philosophy foundational to the services offered?

___ Is the personal philosophy compatible with your values and needs? If not, is this practitioner willing to help you find another who can better meet your needs?

___ Is this practitioner's style of interacting comfortable for you?

___ For services to be helpful, what does this practitioner expect from you?

___ What do the fee schedule and billing guidelines look like?

___ Is this practitioner willing to work with your insurance company?

Consumer Feedback

___ What type of reputation does this practitioner have in the community?

___ Do current or past clients or patients recommend this practitioner?

___ Concerning this practitioner's professional behavior, have any complaints been lodged against him or her?

Spiritual Reflection

Like a shepherd He will tend His flock,
In His arms He will gather the lambs
And carry them in His bosom. (ISAIAH 40:11)

As I write this final chapter I am reminded that it has been a little more than five years since the loss of my brother and father. Shortly after my father died, we made a family pact. Devastated and exhausted after loss's nine-month siege, my mother and I agreed that nobody would have permission to get sick or die for at least five years. As silly as it may seem, we were half serious. We could not imagine surviving further loss. Being more intentional about our relationship and taking better care of ourselves and each other became priorities. When life once again offers us a glimpse of its tenuousness, we remind each other of our pact.

As I look to the future, I know there will be other losses; no promise or pact can protect us from this reality. We must be prepared to embrace life's sorrows as well as its joys. If any good news is to be had, it is that God desires to not only sustain us through the trials we encounter, but He also longs to heal our brokenness and to enrich our life with His love and grace. It is difficult to fathom such extravagant, unconditional love, yet so many of us leave His gift unopened. We admire its wrapping or marvel at its enormity, but avoid getting too close. Something within us cannot grasp the idea that God meant this for us, and so we put conditions on accepting His gift.

The conditions we insist upon typically focus on improving the quality of our personhood, and thus our worthiness to receive God's gift. Some of us worry about our lack of participation in formal religious organizations, so we tell ourselves that we must start attending church; or if we are already actively involved in a church, we must increase our prayer or study time. Others of us focus on a bad habit or destructive behavior we need to eliminate. Perhaps we feel guilty about the difficult spiritual questions we wrestle with, and we don't feel it would be right to accept God's generosity until we have things squared away. Some of us feel unworthy because of a past we are ashamed of. With little hope of ever earning His sacred gift, we can think of nothing that would cover our mistakes and poor choices. Regardless of the conditions with which we saddle ourselves, or the excuses we use for not reaching out, all serve as cumbersome burdens that prevent any possibility of healing.

The day before his death, my father lay in a semi-comatose state. As I sat holding his hand, I could not help but think of the times I had watched him struggle with difficult spiritual issues. I wondered if he had ever come to terms with these or found the peace I longed for him to have. Leaning close, I whispered in his ear, reminding him that it is never too late to reach out to God. We do not have to be ready, or sure, or perfect, or even religious. God is willing to meet us right where we are. His gifts of unconditional love, grace, and healing are all free, no strings attached! Impossible, you say? For us, perhaps—for God, I think not. All we have to do is reach out, take His hand, and allow Him to lift us above the mire. Anything is possible when we surrender our lives to Him.

Imagine yourself reaching out to take God's hand. In your sketchbook, draw a picture or create a collage that represents the feelings you experience as you accept the gifts He offers.

Is there anything keeping you from accepting God's gifts?

If you have identified barriers that prevent you from fully embracing God's acceptance, what kind of plan can you construct to address this issue?

Who can you count on to help you implement your plan?

As you think of good self-care throughout the recovery process, what things would you like to turn over to God? How will you accomplish this?

Meditation

You prepare a table before me. (PSALM 23:5)

Self-care does not have to equal "selfish care." Remember, taking good care of ourselves is always the initial step in gathering the resources we will need to enrich the lives of others. But first, we must find respite from the challenges we encounter as a result of loss. Nourishment for the body, mind, and soul is found in God. The ample feast He spreads before us is meant to renew our strength and refresh our spirits. He bids us to come to His table where there is always a place set . . . just for us.

Summary

You have to dare to stand erect in your struggles. The temptation is to complain, to beg, to be overwhelmed and find your satisfaction in the pity you evoke. But you know already that this is not gaining for you what your heart most desires. As long as you remain standing, you can speak freely to others, reach out to them, and receive from them.[3] HENRI NOUWEN

Learning to take good care of ourselves is a skill worth honing. Despite the whirlwind of factors wearing down our resilience, we have the ability to reach within ourselves to find a means to maintain our balance. In considering physical, emotional, and spiritual aspects of our being, we acknowledge the mind-body connection that is at the apex of holistic health. Reaching beyond ourselves is also an important aspect in the recovery process. In accepting formal assistance through professional health care providers and support groups, we increase opportunities to maximize our physical and emotional well-being. Perhaps the best news of all is that we do not have to accomplish this all on our own. In sharing the challenges of recovery with God, we lighten our burdens by keeping company with Him.

Describe the most surprising thing you discovered about yourself after reading this chapter.

What aspect of self-care seems most helpful to you and why?

Recommended Reading

Chapters 10 and 11 of *A Grace Disguised,* by Gerald Sittser

Chapter 10 of *The Courage to Grieve,* by Judy Tatelbaum

Appendix A

Outline of the Grief Recovery Process

CHAPTER ONE: IDENTIFYING AND NAMING OUR LOSS

1. Defining catastrophic loss
2. The many faces of catastrophic loss
3. Loss and the cascade of loss that may follow
4. The unique aspects of loss and the grieving process
5. Identifying and naming each loss
6. Resiliency characteristics
7. Drawing from spirituality's strength

CHAPTER TWO: OUR INITIAL RESPONSE TO LOSS

1. Reflexive cry of protest
2. Healthy detachment and the use of ego-defense mechanisms
3. Prolonged detachment and potential remedies
4. Education and the grieving process
5. Evaluating consequences of loss
6. Identifying resources for survival and growth
7. Recognizing the social implications of loss
8. Facing difficult spiritual questions

CHAPTER THREE: THE REALIZATION THAT WE ARE FOREVER CHANGED

1. Initial recognition and loss of control
2. Recognizing and understanding our anger
3. Beyond anger: resentment, bitterness, and rage
4. The price we pay for hanging on to our anger
5. A five-step anger resolution process
6. Spirituality and anger: allowing God to relieve us of our burden

CHAPTER FOUR: BARGAINING WITH LOSS AND ITS PAIN

1. Bargaining's place in the grieving process: a normal response
2. Bargaining as a magical protection
3. Exposing the essence of bargaining
4. Broadening our perspective: the purposeful search for loss's gifts
5. Coming to terms with change brought on by loss
6. Accepting loss and trusting God to take care of us

CHAPTER FIVE: ACCEPTING LOSS AND MANAGING THE PAIN THAT FOLLOWS

1. Depression as a normal response to loss
2. The many faces of depression
3. Gauging our degree of concern
4. When to seek immediate professional assistance
5. Three major influences that impact the degree of our depression
6. Other mediating factors and their impact on depression
7. Tools for managing depression
8. Spirituality and the management of depression

CHAPTER SIX: LIFE-CHANGING CHALLENGES ENCOUNTERED IN RECOVERY

1. Recovery and reorganization
2. The experience of aloneness
3. Working through related issues connected to past loss
4. The process of forgiving others
5. Forgiving ourselves
6. Spirituality and the challenge to forgive

CHAPTER SEVEN: INTEGRATION OF LOSS AND JOY'S RENEWAL

1. A picture of integration
2. Understanding the necessary steps in the process of personal transformation
3. Identifying life's essentials
4. Gifts that flow from the lessons of loss
5. Choosing our response to loss
6. The enrichment of life following the experience of loss
7. God as a partner in our journey

CHAPTER EIGHT: TAKING CARE OF OURSELVES IN THE MIDST OF LOSS

1. Learning about self-care
2. Constructing a plan for self-care: our physical needs
3. Establishing healthy boundaries: our emotional needs
4. Finding competent formal therapeutic services
5. Community support groups
6. Creating linkages for enhanced assistance
7. Learning to accept gifts of support from God

Appendix B

Finding Competent, Formal Therapeutic Support

Recommendation of family, friend, or colleague?

Name: _____

Type of practitioner: _____

Contact number: _____

Comments about practitioner: _____

Check the questions whose answers you consider to be essential in your decision-making process. Use a separate piece of paper to record the information you gather.

Education

___ What school(s) did this practitioner attend?

___ Does the school have a good reputation?

___ What accreditation does the school, or program within the school, possess?

___ Related to the services provided, what degree(s) or certification(s) did this practitioner earn?

Training and Practice

___ Does this practitioner have any special training or experience with the issues for which you seek help?

___ Does this practitioner consistently engage in continuing education to keep abreast of changes in his or her field?

Quality Control

___ Is the profession guided by national and/or state standards?

___ Is the practitioner you are considering licensed to practice?

___ Is there a governing body that receives consumer complaints or concerns?

___ In terms of the professional community, is this practitioner a member in good standing?

Personal Philosophy and Business Practices

___ Is this practitioner able to describe the guiding philosophy foundational to the services offered?

___ Is the personal philosophy compatible with your values and needs? If not, is this practitioner willing to help you find another who can better meet your needs?

___ Is this practitioner's style of interacting comfortable for you?

___ For services to be helpful, what does this practitioner expect from you?

___ What do the fee schedule and billing guidelines look like?

___ Is this practitioner willing to work with your insurance company?

Consumer Feedback

___ What type of reputation does this practitioner have in the community?

___ Do current or past clients or patients recommend this practitioner?

___ Concerning this practitioner's professional behavior, have any complaints been lodged against him or her?

Appendix C

Resources for Recovery *(and their related subjects)*

Books

Mitch Albom, *Tuesdays with Morrie* (New York: Doubleday, 1997).
  Death and dying

Patty Duke and Gloria Hochman, *A Brilliant Madness* (New York: Bantam Books, 1992).
  Mental illness

Viktor Frankl, *Man's Search for Meaning* (New York: Simon & Schuster, 1984).
  Loss and existential psychology

Grace Ketterman and David Hazard, *When You Can't Say, "I Forgive You"* (Colorado Springs: NavPress, 2000).
  Learning to forgive

Elizabeth Kubler-Ross, *On Death and Dying* (New York: Simon & Schuster, 1969).
  The individual process and personal response to impending death

John Lee, *Facing the Fire* (New York: Bantam Books, 1993).
  Anger management

C. S. Lewis, *A Grief Observed* (New York: Bantam Books, 1961).
  Personal story of loss

Max Lucado, *In the Grip of Grace* (Dallas: Word Publishing, 1996).
  Christian support

Hope MacDonald, *Letters from Heaven* (Colorado Springs: NavPress, 1998).
  Inspirational fiction

Sherwin B. Nuland, *How We Die: Reflections on Life's Final Chapter* (New York: Vintage Books, 1993).
  Case studies dealing with death

Gilda Radner, *It's Always Something* (New York: Simon & Schuster, 1989).
   Personal story, reflections on her battle with cancer

Lillian Rubin, *Tangled Lives* (Boston: Beacon Press, 2000).
   Personal experience with childhood abuse, recovery, and the aging process

Lillian Rubin, *The Transcendent Child* (San Francisco: HarperPerennial, 1997).
   Case studies; people who have overcome loss as a result of abuse and sociological challenges

Gerald Sittser, *A Grace Disguised* (Grand Rapids, Mich.: Zondervan, 1995).
   Surviving a variety of losses

Lewis Smedes, *Forgive and Forget* (New York: Simon & Schuster, 1986).
   The art of forgiveness

Lewis Smedes, *How Can It Be All Right When Everything Is All Wrong?* (New York: Simon & Schuster, 1986).
   Dealing with life challenges

Judy Tatelbaum, *The Courage to Grieve* (New York: Harper & Row, 1984).
   Death and the grieving process

Philip Yancey, *Where Is God When It Hurts?* (Grand Rapids, Mich.: Zondervan, 1990).
   Loss and spiritual development

Internet

Grief and Loss Resource Center: www.selkirk-tangiers.com/~spirit/grief/grief.html
   Formatted for a variety of losses; resources and links

The Grief Recovery Institute: www.grief-recovery.com
   Recovery issues, articles, and information resources

Grief Recovery Online: www.groww.com
   Focused on loss through death; message board, online chat, and resources

GriefShare: www.griefshare.org
   Christian support groups, reading materials, and general resources

Notes

CHAPTER ONE

1. *American Heritage Dictionary of the English Language,* 3d ed., s.v. "catastrophe," s.v. "loss."

2. Gerald Sittser, *A Grace Disguised* (Grand Rapids, Mich.: Zondervan, 1995), p. 16.

3. Sittser, p. 20.

4. Judy Tatelbaum, *The Courage to Grieve* (New York: Harper & Row, 1984), p. 10.

5. Lewis Smedes, *How Can It Be All Right When Everything Is All Wrong?* (New York: Pocket Books, 1986), p. 11.

6. *American Heritage Dictionary,* 3d ed., s.v. "resiliency."

CHAPTER TWO

1. Judy Tatelbaum, *The Courage to Grieve* (New York: Harper & Row, 1984), p. 25.

2. Gerald Sittser, *A Grace Disguised* (Grand Rapids, Mich.: Zondervan, 1995), p. 32.

3. Philip Yancey, *Where Is God When It Hurts?* (Grand Rapids, Mich.: Zondervan, 1990), p. 95.

4. Lewis Smedes, *How Can It Be All Right When Everything Is All Wrong?* (New York: Pocket Books, 1986), p. 10.

5. Diane Dempsey Marr, *No Need to Be Alone* (Melodies of Love and Grace: Part One, U.S. Copyright Office, Registration Number PAU 948 589, 1987).

CHAPTER THREE

1. *American Heritage Dictionary of the English Language,* 3d ed., s.v. "anger."

2. *American Heritage Dictionary,* 3d ed., s.v. "resentment," s.v. "bitterness," s.v. "rage."

3. Ruth Stapleton, *The Experience of Inner Healing* (Waco, Tex.: Word, 1979), p. 194.

4. Viktor Frankl, *Man's Search for Meaning* (New York: Simon & Schuster, 1984), pp. 98-99.

CHAPTER FOUR

1. Donna Davenport, "A Closer Look at the 'Healthy' Grieving Process," *The Personnel and Guidance Journal*, 59(6), 1981, p. 332.

2. Viktor Frankl, *Man's Search for Meaning* (New York: Simon & Schuster, 1984), p. 116.

3. Lewis Smedes, *How Can It Be All Right When Everything Is All Wrong?* (New York: Pocket Books, 1986), p. 25.

4. Frankl, p. 116.

5. Diane Dempsey Marr, *There Goes Sue* (Melodies of Love and Grace: Part Two, U.S. Copyright Office, Registration Number PAU 946 554, 1987).

CHAPTER FIVE

1. Gerald Sittser, *A Grace Disguised* (Grand Rapids, Mich.: Zondervan, 1995), p. 62.

2. Henri Nouwen, *The Inner Voice of Love* (New York: Image Books, 1998), p. 3.

3. Gerald Corey, *Theory and Practice of Counseling and Psychotherapy: Fifth Edition* (Pacific Grove, Calif.: Brooks/Cole Publishing, 1996).

4. Corey, pp. 338-339.

5. Corey, pp. 320-322.

6. Corey, pp. 322-323.

7. Philip Yancey, *Where Is God When It Hurts?* (Grand Rapids, Mich.: Zondervan, 1990), p. 157.

CHAPTER SIX

1. Philip Yancey, *Where Is God When It Hurts?* (Grand Rapids, Mich.: Zondervan, 1990), p. 173.

2. Lewis Smedes, *Forgive and Forget* (New York: Pocket Books, 1986), p. 60.

3. Smedes, p. 12.

4. Viktor Frankl, *Man's Search for Meaning* (New York: Simon & Schuster, 1984), p. 96.

CHAPTER SEVEN

1. Diane Dempsey Marr, *His Signature of Love* (Melodies of Love and Grace: Part Two, U.S. Copyright Office, Registration Number PAU 946 554, 1987).

2. Mitch Albom, *Tuesdays with Morrie* (New York: Doubleday, 1997), pp. 65-66.

3. James Edwards, *The Divine Intruder* (Colorado Springs: NavPress, 2000), p. 32.

4. Gerald Sittser, *A Grace Disguised* (Grand Rapids, Mich.: Zondervan, 1995), p. 78.

5. Judy Tatelbaum, *The Courage to Grieve* (New York: Harper & Row, 1984), p. 94.

CHAPTER EIGHT

1. Henri Nouwen, *The Inner Voice of Love* (New York: Image Books, 1998), p. 55.

2. Henry Cloud and John Townsend, *Boundaries* (Grand Rapids, Mich.: Zondervan, 1992), p.105.

3. Nouwen, pp. 61-62.

About the Author

DIANE DEMPSEY MARR earned her Ph.D. in counseling and human services from the University of Idaho in 1991. She has been active in her profession for more than twenty years both as a counselor and educator. She serves as professor of counseling and education at Whitworth College, a private Christian liberal arts institution located in the Pacific Northwest, and is coordinator of the Graduate Counseling Program there. Dr. Marr's scholarly efforts include professional publications focused on assessment and treatment support for youth and adults, and the intersection between counseling, alternative medicine, and holistic health care. She has presented her work to international as well as national audiences including the 24th Triennial International Conference of University Women at Stanford University, the International Conference of the Union Gospel Missions, and the World Conference of the American Counseling Association.